A WAKE UP CALL FOR SCHOOLS

A New Order in Public Education

Patricia Anne Duncan Parrish

ROWMAN & LITTLEFIELD EDUCATION

A division of
ROWMAN & LITTLEFIELD PUBLISHERS, INC.
Lanham • New York • Toronto • Plymouth, UK

Published by Rowman & Littlefield Education
A division of Rowman & Littlefield Publishers, Inc.
A wholly owned subsidiary of The Rowman & Littlefield Publishing Group, Inc.
4501 Forbes Boulevard, Suite 200, Lanham, Maryland 20706
http://www.rowmaneducation.com

Estover Road, Plymouth PL6 7PY, United Kingdom

Copyright © 2010 by Patricia Anne Duncan Parrish

All rights reserved. No part of this book may be reproduced in any form or by any electronic or mechanical means, including information storage and retrieval systems, without written permission from the publisher, except by a reviewer who may quote passages in a review.

British Library Cataloguing in Publication Information Available

Library of Congress Cataloging-in-Publication Data
Parrish, Patricia Anne Duncan, 1942–
  A wake up call for schools : a new order in public education / Patricia Anne Duncan Parrish.
    p. cm.
  Includes bibliographical references.
  ISBN 978-1-60709-704-4 (cloth : alk. paper) — ISBN 978-1-60709-705-1 (pbk. : alk. paper) — ISBN 978-1-60709-706-8 (electronic)
  1. Public schools—United States. 2. Educational accountability—United States. 3. Education and state—United States. 4. Educational change—United States. I. Title.
LA217.2.P37 2010
370.973—dc22
                                                  2010015923

∞™ The paper used in this publication meets the minimum requirements of American National Standard for Information Sciences—Permanence of Paper for Printed Library Materials, ANSI/NISO Z39.48-1992.

Printed in the United States of America

DEDICATION

This book is dedicated to gallant warriors and gentle giants from the classroom to the central office

- who are empowered and empowering in their unrelenting vision and high expectations for educational excellence in every classroom,
- who through their perseverance and positive influence honor hallowed halls of educational institutions in this country and worldwide,
- who hold their heads high and their backs straight and strong in the face of arrows of mediocrity,
- who step up to the plate of public education day after day after day knowing quantifiable, higher-level educational standards for every student are a global priority and a national emergency,
- who model dignity for every individual—red, yellow, black, and white (and brown?)!,
- who kneel to gently touch and humbly lift the spirit of a child—every child—every child.

This book is, also, dedicated to citizens of the universe who are unrelenting in unified commitment with educators to collaboratively produce our mutual goal—an educated citizenry equipped with skills to function successfully in the rigorous marketplace of the international twenty-first century—and beyond.

All of this will not be finished in the first 100 days, nor will it be finished in the first 1,000 days, . . . nor even perhaps in our lifetime on this planet, but let us begin.

—John Fitzgerald Kennedy, 1960

CONTENTS

LIST OF FIGURES AND TABLES		vii
FOREWORD		ix
ACKNOWLEDGMENTS		xi
1	THE CLEARING	1
2	THE GREAT DIVIDE	9
3	THE PLAN	17
4	THE PAINTBRUSH	23
5	BILLY	31
6	RED, YELLOW, BLACK, AND WHITE (AND BROWN?)!	43
7	THE Y IN THE ROAD	55
8	TEDDY	61

CONTENTS

9	THE TRIAD	71
10	A NEW ORDER	85
NOTES		101
BIBLIOGRAPHY		107
ABOUT THE AUTHOR		113

FIGURES AND TABLES

LIST OF FIGURES

Figure 3.1.	District and Campus Site-based Decision-making Teams—A Seamless Continuum	19
Figure 3.2.	District and Campus Mission Statements—A Seamless Continuum	20
Figure 3.3.	District and Campus Site-based Decision-making Process—A Seamless Continuum	21
Figure 9.1.	The Triad—Home, School, Community	72

LIST OF TABLES

Table 1.1.	Comparison of School Readiness—Student A and Student B	5
Table 7.1.	Life Span: Birth through Age Eighty	56

FOREWORD

All of my professional life has been spent working with children. As a teacher, principal, superintendent, and later as an executive director for a nonprofit organization that provided services to special needs children, I have seen it all: the good, the bad, and the ugly . . . especially the ugly. As I read and reread Patricia Anne Duncan Parrish's book, I thought how wonderful it would have been if all of us in the kid business had followed her enlightened pathway. What a difference we would have made. This book has positive implications for not only educators but all who work with children: youth counselors, social workers, and even volunteers who offer services to children.

I have known Dr. Parrish for more than twenty years and have watched her perform miracles in schools. I was so fortunate to have her join us in a district where I was superintendent. What Dr. Parrish accomplished was truly amazing. Complaints from parents were resolved and our biggest critics became our greatest supporters. But even more important was the complete change of attitude that took place in the district. It was truly miraculous. And this is directly attributable to the leadership Dr. Parrish provided. So when she writes about improvement and moving us

FOREWORD

ahead, she does not do it from the ivory tower; she writes from experience with boots solidly on the ground!

I know you will find this book one of the best you have read. If I were still in the business, I would make it required reading for everyone in the district.

Jack Shanks
teacher, principal, superintendent, executive director,
Texas Elks Children's Services, Inc.

ACKNOWLEDGMENTS

Each individual in a global society functions individually, yet collectively. The image of innumerable gallant warriors and gentle giants comes before me now. To each of these educators with whom I have labored in unison on behalf of young people, I express my deepest gratitude. At this time I gratefully acknowledge specifically the following.

- Thomas F. Koerner, PhD, vice president and editorial director, Rowman & Littlefield Publishers, Inc., the Education Division, for his guidance through the writing and completion of this book
- Three professional colleagues who read every page of this book during its development, offering comments and recommendations for improvement in format and content
    1. James A. Vornberg, PhD—professor, Department of Educational Leadership; director, Meadows Principal Improvement Program; former department head and former interim dean, College of Education and Human Services, Texas A&M University–Commerce—co-author/editor,

ACKNOWLEDGMENTS

Texas Public School Organization and Administration and *The New School Leader for the 21st Century: The Principal*—instructional and administrative positions in education in Missouri, Texas, Arizona, and Brazil

2. Ron Golden, MEd—coordinator of educator preparation, Texas A&M University-Commerce Navarro Partnership—more than thirty years in campus-based instructional and administrative positions in public education—supervisor in teacher education at the postsecondary level—technical advisor through the Texas Education Agency in low-performing schools—campus administrator mentor for compliance with federal rules and regulations through No Child Left Behind

3. Jane Reisman, PhD—president, Organizational Research Services, Seattle, Washington, develops outcome-based strategic plans and evaluation systems in public, non-profit, and private organizations, including theory of change, logic models, and data collection—former faculty member, Ohio State University and Pacific Lutheran University—author, *Outcomes for Success!* and *A Guide to Measuring Advocacy and Policy*—received 2001 Best Sociological Practice Award from Society of Applied Sociologists

Educational institutions are as effective as the strength of the triad—school, home, community. In addition to the multiples of gallant warriors and gentle giants in public education who step up to the plate on behalf of students every day, I express sincere appreciation to the homes, the families who expectantly trust educators with their greatest treasures—their children. I am, also, deeply grateful to community members who join hands with educators in the development of training programs designed to meet the needs and demands of the twenty-first-century marketplace—from global industries of Phillips Petroleum Company,

ACKNOWLEDGMENTS

Dow Chemical Company, BASF, and others to small business owners in local communities.

I thank students in my classes, grades one through twelve—for the ones who got away, for the ones who arrived at the schoolhouse every day—whose vivid, heart-wrenching stories enrich this writing. Their penetrating influence on me as an educator is now passed to readers of my book—profound messages—promises we must keep.

Recognition is extended to professors of Texas A&M University-Commerce with whom I instruct each semester—for the excellence and depth of their knowledge and for their keen sense of leadership and mentorship with postsecondary education students. Commendation is extended to enrolled university students who sharpen the axe of their skill base of educational excellence so each may indeed positively impact citizens of all ages—from early childhood through adulthood—in this nation and in the international society of the twenty-first century.

Specifically, I am deeply grateful to my family—one who was beside me before I entered my first teaching position, most who were birthed during the journey.

- Linden J. Parrish, EdD—the little boy in the life-changing third-grade class of Ms. Lawrence—educator for more than four decades in instructional positions in K-12 public schools in Texas and in New York, in instructional positions in postsecondary education, in campus and district instructional leadership, and in superintendent positions in public schools in Texas.
- My children and grandchildren—Phillip, Timothy, Stephen, Mitzy, Kristy, Stanford, Jefferson, Bailee, Joseph, Caroline, Alexander, Ryan, Landon—the light of the world, as is each mother's child—global citizens of the twenty-first century and beyond, a time I can only see faintly now, a time in which they and our progeny will live.

1

THE CLEARING

As I approached the clearing, I saw them—three shabbily dressed children—two young girls with matted hair that hadn't been combed in days and one little boy—hunkered together under one filthy, frayed blanket, two adult females clothed shoddily, as well. I had driven from the elementary campus in the bitter cold of a frigid winter morning in northeast Texas. Three children were habitually absent, day after day after day. Documented communications with their caregivers were unsuccessful no home telephone number, unanswered mail. Today I had a sketchy, incomplete map scribbled on crinkled notebook paper to guide me in locating these children.

The first miles in my quest were smooth—paved two-lane roads with center stripes, generous shoulders flowing smoothly onto well-manicured Bermuda grass from the last mow prior to winter settling in. It was a particularly chilling winter—drizzling, drizzling cold, steady rain for days on end, temperatures hovering thirty-three to thirty-five degrees during the days, teasing temperatures below freezing during frosty nights.

Dairymen and ranchers mumbled in low, guttural growls, their warm breaths blowing serendipitous billows of vapor with each

CHAPTER 1

grumble. "Ever' morning for days I've been out 'fore daybreak breaking ice in them ponds so the livestock can have water to drink. We haven't had 'northerns' like this since I was a kid." Sleet pelted the countryside through the night as mammas placed extra covers on the little ones so they wouldn't "catch a fright of cold."

A lopsided arrow on my hand-drawn map indicated a right turn about a half mile up the road. I activated the blinker, as if a car were behind me. Actually, I hadn't seen a vehicle for miles. The right turn was onto a "blacktop" maintained by the county—no shoulders on either side—so narrow that cars, trucks, and farm equipment passing beside necessitated one vehicle dropping its wheels off the right side onto northeast Texas red, gummy clay so the other could gingerly pass.

I claimed the middle of the road—no motor transportation in sight, ahead nor behind, a squirrel scampering across in front, red, bushy tail fluttering like a wind-whipped flag. The northeast Texas woods intensified with each mile. If the sun peeped from the clouds, its brilliance was quickly lost in tangled poison oak, blackberry vines, gnarled trees—likely no one had walked these woods in years. I stopped at the crossroad—had to turn right or left. I glanced again at the crumpled map. Turn left.

Within a few hundred yards the dreaded sign for lone drivers indicated the "paved" road extended for one-half mile. Thump! Gently pressing the brake, I dropped onto red clay riddled with ruts from farm equipment chug-a-lugging through this desolate connector of humanity. Faint scribbles on the map indicated to turn right at the first mailbox. The box hung loosely by one square head nail, the post leaning to the left—had likely been bumped by the neighbor's tractor months before, partially hidden now in tangled, knee-high weeds. "Don't receive much mail out here 'no how' . . . no need to tack it up . . ."

I turned right onto two jagged ruts through the field—one for each set of wheels, gripping the steering wheel. My knuckles reddened and ached from the grasp. Last night's sleet remained moist—too dangerous to steer out of the ruts—tall Dallas grass whipping at my windows. . . . And ahead, the clearing . . . the children! I pulled my heavy winter coat tightly to my neck, gasping at the first breath of wet, frigid winter air.

The pungent fragrance of an early morning campfire floated toward my nostrils. I began the walk of solitude from the safety of my vehicle to the children, the adult females, and the campfire—my every measured step watched intensely through hollowed, faint eyes of the huddled, bent ones in the clearing—step, step, one step at a time.

I briefly introduced myself, stammering, as a representative from the school. One by one each stated his/her name, softly, briefly, first names only. With the early morning bite of cold, I questioned their huddling around the campfire instead of being in the warmth of the run-down, unpainted shanty that was their apparent abode. "No heat in the house, no fireplace. Can't build a fire inside. Burn the house down. Sleep inside at night. Stay warm by fire outside when sun's up."

And so it was! And so it was! An educator had cautiously, one hesitant step followed by another, unveiled, entered into, another culture . . . with its rituals, heroines—so incredibly different from her own—not greater nor less—but so incredibly different. Benjamin Bloom, Abraham Maslow, and other prominent philosophers and educational leaders darted to and fro, spasmodically, through my thoughts as I very, very cautiously—speaking ever so softly—moved closer and closer toward the huddled children, the bent adults, and the campfire—into a culture where I had never been, having come from my air-conditioned, well-coiffed, fragrantly perfumed civilization. I stood alone in their culture—at their mercy—alone.

Fortunately for me, standing alone on a drizzling, icy, winter morn in the clearing occurred during my early years in education. Having served in varying positions as an educator for more than

CHAPTER 1

thirty years—extending from classroom teaching in schools in the rural countryside to highly populated areas fifty miles east of New York City . . . diagnostic services in multiples of schools . . . central office administration in districts in the geographic area of the fourth-largest city in the nation . . . university-level instruction—I consider the unveiling of this culture—so startlingly different from my own—as one of the most mountaintop, poignant revelations of my career. It is likely the clearing has charted my path and passion for reaching all children, possibly more deeply and more intrinsically than I am aware.

With frequency I reflect on the hollow eyes of the huddled children around the campfire, on the faint, squinting eyes of the emaciated adults, likely taking care of business as usual, as it had been taken care of for generations, one generation after another after another after another. When children and adults are hungry, cold, fearful, apprehensive, they function in survival mode, grasping for necessities of life upon which to sustain themselves. Learning skills to equip oneself for a better life is not a priority. Sufficient food for sustenance is.

When educators reach for children within their natural cultures, we readily become aware that deprivation of spirit, of expectation, of cognizance is repeated in schools throughout the United States—large schools, small schools, rural schools, urban schools. Approximately 12 to 17 percent of U.S. citizens live below the poverty threshold in one of the most industrialized countries in the world. In the United States children are most likely the ones living in poverty.[1] The ravages of the recession experienced in this nation result in more citizens being swallowed toward and into poverty.

> More than any other factor, poverty accounts for poor school performance. Race and ethnicity are related to poverty.[2]

Although national high school dropout rates, generally, have decreased from the twentieth into the twenty-first century, ap-

THE CLEARING

proximately 30 percent of high school students leave school prior to graduation ill equipped to survive the rigors of the international marketplace of the twenty-first century.[3] During this century one-third of African American minors (less than eighteen years of age) live below the poverty threshold.[4] Teachers unequivocally hold the torch of light and illuminating hope through which young people may gain skills and be elevated to a higher level of functioning in this century.

Students enter kindergarten with differing levels of readiness, to a great extent a reflection of their preschool culture. Imagine Student A and Student B. It is the first day of school. The yellow school bus has transported the final group of students on this crisp autumn morning—from the culture of their home to expectations and rituals of school culture. Within a few hours yellow buses reverse the process—from the school to the home—back and

Table 1.1. Comparison of School Readiness—Student A and Student B

Student A	Student B
Fifth birthday last October	Fifth birthday week before first day of school
Parents completed college	Parents dropped out of high school
Both parents age thirty+ at birth of child	Both parents seventeen at birth of child
Knows letters of alphabet, beginning to read*	No exposure to alphabet, text-deprived home*
Writes name in legible print	Doesn't know how to hold pencil, crayon
Enrolled in preschool program at age three	No preschool academic, social instruction
Travels extensively nationally and internationally	Has not been out of the neighborhood
Received first computer at age three	No technology exposure
Total family annual income at $175,000+	Lives in poverty, frequent parental unemployment

*Research reported in the New York Times indicates vocabularies of children of professional parents include approximately twice the number of words as vocabularies of children whose parents receive federal assistance (1,100 words/525 words).[5]

CHAPTER 1

forth, back and forth, day after day after day—from one planet in the solar system to another—the home culture, the school culture. Again, imagine Student A and Student B on their first day in kindergarten.

Effective educators look in the mirror, turning to the right, grimacing to the left, smiling, frowning. Do we view our reflections through shaded eyes, querying ourselves? Am I the saint, or am I the villain?

- Do my students learn because of me, or is the learning of my students compromised as a result of instruction I provide?
- Am I the pathway to a productive, fulfilling life for my students, or am I the hurdle?
- Do I truly, unconditionally, reach for every child and lift each gently, expectantly, to higher levels of functioning?
- Do I greet all children by name—Juan, Phillipe, Sara, Consuela?
- Do I call on each child equitably—irrespective of gender, ethnicity, odor, cultural values, socioeconomic level, diversity?
- Do I challenge all children to function at higher levels of Bloom's Taxonomy—all children?
- Do I unabashedly rejoice as every student enters my classroom for the unique intellectual, genetic, cellular, emotional constellation each is?

Move closer to the mirror—closer. Describe qualities the reflection in the mirror reveals. Critique. Begin now. Assess those dynamics within you that must be amended so you will cherish and elevate each student who enters your classroom, your school, your district. Fashion new again—every day—your commitment to be a shining torch for children—truly, the hope of the world! Contemplate—if not me, then who? If not my grade level/

department team, then whose team? If not my school, then which school?

The clock is ticking—day after day after day. Children come. Children go. The time is brief. Positively impact humanity now, today, during these developmental years. A call for action in public education is a critical, national, international priority. It begins with the reflection in the mirror . . .

2

THE GREAT DIVIDE

Cross-cultural dissonance—the mismatch between the culture of the student and the culture of the educator—the great divide—is the discord at the stream's crossing. Cross-cultural dissonance is one of the greatest contributors to public school mediocrity and decay in this century—the great divide. Data published in 2007–2008 by the National Center for Education Statistics, United States Department of Education, indicate approximately 42 percent of students enrolled in public schools in this nation represent minority ethnicities; 83 percent of teachers during the same time period represent the white ethnicity—multicultural education, or cross-cultural dissonance.[1]

When kindergarten students jump from the school bus—Asian, African American, Hispanic, white, male, female, disabled, poverty-stricken, wealthy—eager for their first day of school, dissonance squelches. Cross-cultural dissonance is an insidious germ that infiltrates every action, verbal and nonverbal, of those it afflicts. It permeates the classroom. It permeates the hall. It permeates parent-teacher conferences. Parents sense it. Students sense it—and subsequently wither from it. Professional colleagues

CHAPTER 2

shrink from it or, forbid, join the chorus! It dissolves entire instructional programs—mediocrity to decay.

Kevin stole my heart. Yes, he did—a small-built fourth grader, sandy blond hair, musty odor, one eye—one eye. . . . The other socket steadied an artificial eye, a result of a childhood accident—so timid he hardly lifted his head. The two eyes, almost the same blue hue, gazed in noticeably differing positions. He spoke in a whisper, only when addressed by another—either peer or adult. Kevin was within the tutelage of a colleague in the reading lab, her table positioned across the room from mine. The lab, located in the basement of a deteriorating multistory building, was dedicated to students—third and fourth graders—who struggled in reading and language arts.

Every day, Monday through Friday, 2:30 p.m. to 3:20 p.m., disheveled students entered the lab, downcast, bumping each other—in and out, in and out, in and out. Kevin entered, downtrodden, no eye contact, sitting at his assigned table, same chair, same table, every day, 2:30 p.m. to 3:20 p.m., in and out, propping his pale head on his left arm. "Boys and girls, open your reader to page 157," each student in numbing file day after day after day orally reading three pages, then the next child, then the next—around the table—every day—day after day.

I shuddered from the other side of the lab day after day after day—in the basement in the deteriorating building called a school. After Kevin struggled through words on his assigned pages, little if any comprehension, the next student in monotone commenced to read . . . and the next . . . and the next . . .

Kevin nodded sleepily, his head bobbing up and down like a cork. Ms. Bowen stood up at the end of the table—where she sat, day after day after day after day. She vaulted, yelling full throttle Kevin's name, stomping as she approached the frightened child. She launched into hitting him with the palm of her hand repeatedly across his back.

I trembled, weakening and nauseated, turning to my assigned students, "Boys and girls, let's focus on our assignment"—in the reading lab in the basement of the deteriorating building called a school. Cross-cultural dissonance! Look at the reflection in the mirror.

Poverty in itself is a culture—early multiple pregnancies, minimal if any prenatal and infant care, unemployment, food stamps, malnourishment, single-parent households, despair, overcrowded housing. Demographics are shuffling, as cards in a deck. The Hispanic population continues to be the largest minority group in the United States. The second largest minority group is the African American population. The most rapidly growing ethnic group in the nation is the Hispanic population.[2]

The nation is evolving, is elevating to another rung. To what extent are educators rising up to meet diverse needs of the kaleidoscope of twenty-first-century learners? For educational institutions to succeed in producing an educated citizenry, educators must function in unison, must increase awareness of characteristics and needs of twenty-first-century learners—and characteristics and needs of the twenty-first-century international marketplace.

Only those who relish this challenge are prepared for the stewardship of educating young people during this era in the history of this nation. The countries of the universe are moving forward into pathways that have not been traversed by previous generations. It is inherent educators step up to the plate with knowledge necessary to equip students with skills to survive profitably into and through this uncharted course.

It was midmorning. Each student assumed a responsibility for the luncheon scheduled for tomorrow. It was our first fundraising activity. A previous clothing project resulted in each student's red-checked apron to wear during luncheons. The city inspector verified our commercial food preparation equipment met sanitation standards.

CHAPTER 2

Handwritten invitations by enrolled students to each faculty member were sent the week before. Reminders were placed in boxes yesterday. "Faculty luncheon will be served in foods lab on October 5th, 11:00 a.m.–12:30 p.m., tossed salad, choice of dressings, baked chicken, scalloped potatoes, sautéed green beans with almond slivers, homemade rolls, assortment of cobblers, tea, coffee @ $1.25." We scurried about with last-minute details—furniture arranged, dough prepared for dinner rolls. A knock sounded at the door.

Mr. Bashinski, counselor, asked to speak with me. Glancing back to ensure all students were productively executing assigned preparation tasks, I hesitantly stepped into the hall.

Middle school students enrolled in this course had been hand selected by counseling and administrative staff. Students entered with a plethora of characteristics of concern—potential school dropouts, academic skills below grade level, lower socioeconomic status, frequent disciplinary referrals, one or more retentions, inadequate social skills. An intensive effort to regain students' interest in school (and equip them with saleable skills if efforts were unsuccessful) was launched throughout the state. My training and subsequent certification for this unique, challenging assignment had been completed during the previous summer.

Next fall these students were scheduled to enroll in the local high school when dropout may likely occur prior to graduation. It typically did. Year after year students exhibiting these histories disappeared from the educational system between middle school and high school—a personal and national tragedy. Others entered high school and dropped out quickly—older (resulting from elementary school retentions), restless, resentful secondary-level students. What goes around comes around—many lost, lost opportunities for reaching children, for educating students.

"Yes, Mr. Bashinski." "It's necessary to withdraw some of these students from this course. Enrolled minority percentages exceed recommended program ethnicity parameters." I glanced into the room, each student actively engaged in assigned responsibilities, the dough receiving its hourly kneading, clean, steaming dishes being removed from the commercial dishwasher.

I cannot recall if I had ever noticed minorities and nonminorities (white) were enrolled in this course—and that minorities exceeded "recommended program ethnicity parameters." Probably, but not necessarily, I noticed varying colors of skin (and dialect) on the first day of class. But then quickly, no later than the second day of class, each student's name was embedded in my memory with color of skin, dialect, and other characteristics repositioning themselves lower in level of importance.

However, slouching in chairs, surliness in affect, unkempt appearance, lack of eye contact, loud, popping gum (which was known to be prohibited on school property) raised their ugly heads for weeks—a continual testing ground between tutor and tutee. A wall mirror had intentionally been installed so bedraggled students could groom themselves between classes. I remember vividly with glee the first time I glanced toward the mirror where several students were checking their hair, collars, faces. It was a step toward victory that these sullen, disarrayed students were claiming ownership for their appearance.

From the hall I peered closely—nine African Americans, one Hispanic, and one white. Certainly, "recommended program ethnicity parameters" had been exceeded. I motioned for Mr. Bashinski to come closer to the door and observe with me. "Now, Mr. Bashinski, tell me. Which students are you planning to withdraw from this course?" He dismissed himself, never to discuss again with me the importance of selecting students for designated courses based upon "recommended program ethnicity parameters" rather than on documented and apparent needs.

Prior to the close of the school year each student in this course— yes, those who slouched, exhibited surliness, were unkempt,

CHAPTER 2

popped gum, demonstrating minimal if any eye contact at the beginning of the year—presented a fashion show at the country club for one of the local civic clubs. Their grace was flawless. Prior to boarding the bus to ride to the club the superintendent remarked, "Ensure they behave like they're in the country club, not in the country."[3] They behaved as regal kings and queens.

Educators are well reminded to pause a while and reflect on our own behaviors in establishing equitable learning environments for all students. For a designated time period (scheduled class session), return to the looking glass. Reflect on questioning, praise, wait time, reminders, reprimands you demonstrate and implement with and toward your students.

Is the soil fertile for all students to participate equitably? Analyze distribution of higher-level questions by gender, by ethnicity.[4] Weigh implications of your behaviors on classroom climate, on student participation, on student achievement. Dr. Michael Hinojosa, superintendent of the Dallas Independent School District, the twelfth-largest district in the nation, encourages educators to turn on youth—all youth—to learning.

> I'm an immigrant child. My parents had a formal 3rd grade education. People make excuses . . . but I don't buy it. There are a lot of little Michael Hinojosas running around this city waiting for somebody to turn them on.[5]

To what extent are you executing definitive steps "to turn them on"? In preparation for chapter 3 and the development of the schoolwide action plan, consider your values about the following in a multicultural society.

- Equity for all . . . or . . . predetermined societal levels of individual opportunity
- Cherished traditions, cultural pluralism . . . or . . . the melting pot of humanity

- Individual success . . . or . . . team success
- Allegiance to society as a whole . . . or . . . allegiance to identified ethnicity, neighborhood
- Capturing differences . . . or . . . shunning differences
- Achievement *as* life goal . . . or . . . achievement *toward* life goal

The twenty-first century is rigorous, unrelenting, competitive—the century into which our students are catapulted upon high school graduation. To what extent am I, an educator, aware of the dynamics of this era, a nanosecond arena? Effective educators unite and march forth together, arm in arm, in wisdom, in forethought, and in knowledge in the cadence of this century—leaders of humanity, sculptors of children. It is our privilege and unconditional responsibility to equip the progeny in this nation with basic survival skills and the intellectual and emotional repertoire for profitable sustainment in a civilization that reveres the best, the brightest, the strongest in spirit.

Admittedly, it may not be the steps we learned, but the universal band is playing twenty-first-century songs, and we must dance to the beat with urgency! The children are waiting . . .

3

THE PLAN

For an entity to know if it is accomplishing its goals it is imperative investors and investees establish priority criteria toward which it is reaching. Albert Einstein guides us to a higher elevation of reasoning, individually and institutionally.

> The significant problems we face cannot be solved at the same level of thinking we were at when we created them. . . . To raise new questions, new possibilities, to regard old problems from a new angle requires creative imagination and marks real advances.[1]

The vehicle through which new possibilities emerge is the mutually supported, seamless mission continuum of the district and of each campus in the district. This continuum—through aligned mission statements—is the arrow that propels achievement of each enrolled student—in the classroom, on the campus, in the district. Imagine the contagion of enthusiasm that envelops the district as this arrow of a unified mission permeates every classroom. Broadcast online, in print, on the radio, through television, in student backpacks encouraging communitywide input.

CHAPTER 3

The trajectory of the district opens "new questions, new possibilities" for meeting needs and demands of the twenty-first century through education. Embracing knowledge-age challenges from innovative angles—disregarding irrelevant, threadbare rituals—stimulates the district and each of its stakeholders into the new era of effective twenty-first-century educational institutions.

During this awakening, capture each submitted idea. Encourage suppositions—what if?—from all staff—administrative, instructional, custodial/maintenance, food services, transportation. Query students. Include brainstorming in every classroom. Unified we tread forward together as each claims ownership for the process and the product.

As the awakening elevates to a call for action, establish district and campus committees. Synergy explodes throughout the district, onto each campus, into every classroom. Site-based decision-making teams include representation of student diversity, including socioeconomic status. Membership of campus and district teams embodies, but is not limited to, parents, instructional staff, administration, auxiliary services (custodial/maintenance, food services, transportation), small business, industry, agencies, and community.

Initial commission of each campus team and the district team is seamless building and aligning of the mission of the district and each campus—the strategic arrow. Identify characteristics of the product, the beneficiary of this action—an educated citizen. Define this product in data-driven, measurable terms. Examine competencies the product must demonstrate to function successfully in the rigors of the twenty-first century. Encapsulate these competencies into the direction of each mission statement—district and campus.

Action plans, spearheading mutually supporting mission statements through classrooms, campuses, the district, and the community, are fluid, accountable, and amiable to revision based upon formative and summative assessments. The district team and campus teams

THE PLAN

Figure 3.1. District and Campus Site-based Decision-making Teams—A Seamless Continuum

- develop goals and objectives based upon needs assessment,
- implement measurable strategies,
- appropriate resources,
- determine individuals responsible,
- establish timelines,
- schedule formative and summative evaluation,
- revise and realign goals and objectives based upon ongoing needs assessment.[2]

CHAPTER 3

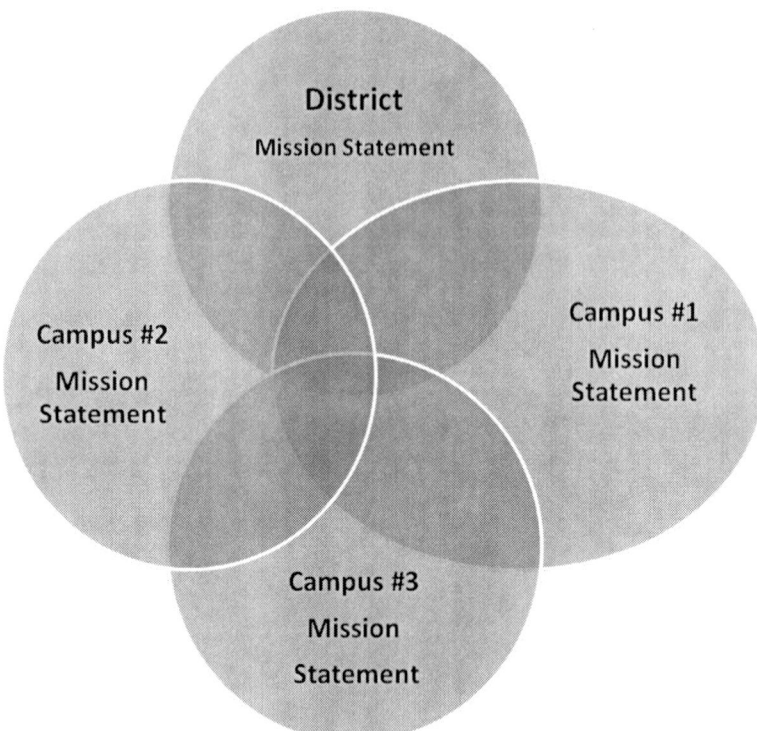

Figure 3.2. District and Campus Mission Statements—A Seamless Continuum

The momentum for new possibilities, creative imagination, and real advances in public education is in motion—moving definitively forward. Campuses and districts expand breadth and depth of action planning, maximizing localization and stakeholder ownership of district and campus missions toward identified goals and objectives resulting in a critical national priority—an educated twenty-first-century citizenry.

> In each century since the beginning of the world wonderful things have been discovered. . . . At first people refuse to believe that a strange new thing can be done, then they begin to hope it can be

THE PLAN

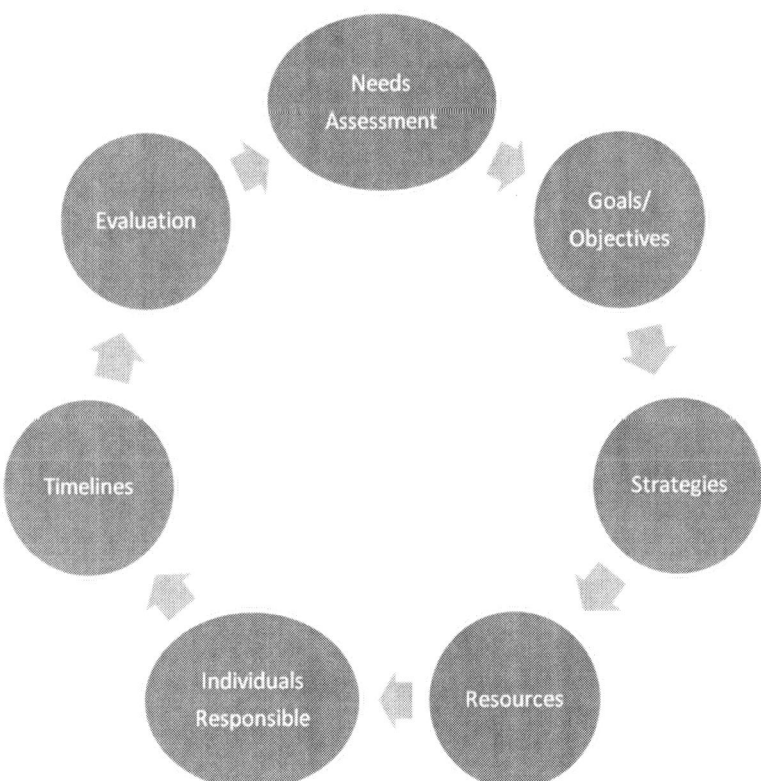

Figure 3.3. District and Campus Site-based Decision-making Process—A Seamless Continuum

done, then they see it can be done—then it is done, and all the world wonders why it was not done centuries ago.[3]

As the locomotive of revolutionary change rolls through each district in the nation—onto every campus—into each classroom—a pivotal component of this momentum is highly qualified personnel maintaining cutting-edge standards of excellence and knowledge year after year after year—through twenty-first-century professional development—the paintbrush.

4

THE PAINTBRUSH

> The foundation of everything is training. . . . Training is the way that gets you there. . . . You can tell people all day long how to do something, and they can read about it and study it, but they have to live it. You have to put the paintbrush in their hand.[1]

Active professional development separates schools that work from other schools. When professional development is meaningful and relevant, participants claim ownership of content and concepts. Preassessment identifies training needs and goals. Postassessment confirms the extent needs are met and goals are reached.

Schools that work nurture a climate of positive, productive, calculable, ongoing change based upon measurable assessment of needs reflected in campus and district improvement plans. Schools that work move forward together. Teaching occurs in concentrated union with others.

> I cannot improve my craft in isolation from others. To improve I must have formats, structures, and plans for reflecting on, changing, and assessing my practice [which] . . . must be continually tested and upgraded with my colleagues.[2]

CHAPTER 4

Educators may muse that content in this chapter does not reflect professional development they have experienced. It minimally reflects professional development I have experienced in more than thirty years in education. It is critical that educators, with students, parents, community members, and business and industry, disrobe shackles of ineffective professional development and with vigor move day by day toward the light of invigorating, meaningful twenty-first-century trainings that envelop the entirety of the school culture.

Unrelenting, expecting, unforgiving, universal twenty-first-century marketplace standards set the stage and establish the pace for excellence in education. Success characteristics of effective professional development leave in the dust the flickering flame of typically occurring training. The flicker of mediocrity explodes into brilliant light when dynamic twenty-first-century trained professionals educate students in twenty-first-century institutions of learning.

Characteristics of effective professional development emulate the following.

- Effective professional development is focused on and measured by achievement of all students—and their incalculable potential.
- Effective professional development is modeled, lead, supported, and expected by administration.
- Effective professional development is appropriated in campus and district budgets, included in campus and district action plans.
- Effective professional development exemplifies research-based characteristics of the adult learner.
- Effective professional development is planned and monitored by its participants based upon immediate short-term and long-term needs.

- Effective professional development is ongoing with sufficient scheduled sessions to support exemplary levels of functioning of educators and students.
- Effective professional development is flexible, encouraging engaging, stimulating dialogue with applicability of content in the classroom.
- Effective professional development trains trainers, encouraging and sustaining—day by day, week by week, month by month—collaboration, mentoring of new teachers by seasoned teachers, team study groups, collegiality of stakeholders.
- Effective professional development acknowledges and celebrates diversity in staff and diversity in students.
- Effective professional development capitalizes on active participatory involvement with parents and community, seizes tested processes and procedures of business and industry for incorporation into razor-sharp, strategic, accountable schools.
- Effective twenty-first-century professional development incorporates technology, the communication and knowledge tools of the new international age.

Through effective professional development the army of professionals is elevated to higher levels of instructional expertise and accountability. A groundswell erupts in which educators eagerly and expectantly pursue research and select data-based strategies that work. A sense of urgency permeates the school environment—every moment a fleeting moment for instruction. Effective professional development sweeps the district with enthusiasm, with vigor, with commitment. Effective professional development is the way. It is the lightning rod for change in educational institutions.

Now return to each listed characteristic of effective professional development. Place a check by each that definitively exemplifies

CHAPTER 4

training provided in your school. Compare and contrast results with school climate, staff morale, community support, and student achievement.

The instructional leader, the building principal, is the key to effective professional development on each campus, exercising the potential of this position for change in rekindling the flickering flame of school climate, staff morale, community support, and student achievement by emblazoning the dimness with the beacon of positive professional development on behalf of young people.

As the light of visionary leadership and site-based decision making emerges through the corridors of the school, build upon, nurture, and dedicate personal and professional energies for growth. Create districtwide communications highlighting emerging synergy that paves the way for positive school climate, invigorated staff morale, communitywide support, and unprecedented measurable improvement in student achievement. Collaborate. Coteach. Mentor. Align horizontal and vertical curricula. Support. Celebrate.

> Members of the good-to-great teams tend to become and remain friends for life. . . . Their experiences went beyond just mutual respect (which they certainly had) to lasting comradeship. . . . The people we interviewed from the good-to-great companies clearly loved what they did, largely because they loved who they did it with.[3]

The superintendent appeared at my office unannounced. I eagerly invited him in, moving from behind my desk so we were positioned side by side. Actually, side-by-side communication is my mode in conferences. Desks are hard and rectangular, having rigid, pointed edges that impede clean-to-the-bone communication. From his affect and stride I sensed this would be clean-to-the-bone.

THE PAINTBRUSH

To this day I am more hesitant to engage in free-flowing dialogue when I am the one positioned on the other side of the desk. (Imagine creativity that is stifled, possibly lost forever, when professionals are barricaded on opposite [opposing?] sides of the hard, oversized desk in the corner office.) Side-by-side communication opens doors, originates and illuminates ideas, designs pathways of success.

Upon employment in the district I quickly learned special education programs had been and continued to be under intense scrutiny as a result of vividly described parental concerns. I subsequently learned the name of the district was frequently spoken irreverently as angered parents took their plights of dissatisfaction, dismay, and disgust to the state education agency.

"Dr. Parrish, during the current school year a thorough, data-driven, in-district monitoring of all special education programs in the district will be conducted. The foundation upon which this process will be based is the state monitoring document for public schools. I'm appointing you to lead this endeavor and serve as my designee in its operations. Develop a strategic plan and a definitive timeline for implementation. Contact my office immediately to schedule an appointment in which we review the step-by-step plan you have developed. Are there any questions?"

I was speechless. I had no questions. I was unsure if a copy of the state monitoring document was in the district. I had not seen one. My first step was to locate it, a product I had not previously reviewed. Yes, there it is in the cabinet in my office. I pulled it from the shelf and dusted it. I then embraced it, suspecting it would be my daily companion for the remainder of my employment in the district. It was.

Endorsing "what's good for the goose is good for the gander" (surely during my weaker moments), I prepared an extensive graphic continuum of in-district monitoring using every indicator in the state monitoring system, exponentially magnifying the initial directive from the superintendent. Each instructional program in the district was included in my plan for an unprecedented indicator-by-indicator review and housecleaning. In addition, through my plan campus and district site-based decision making would be elevated to meet rules and regulations of the state legislature.

During my first year of employment in the district this historic schoolwide monitoring system was implemented. I was at the helm. The purpose was twofold—the first fold being to determine if indeed habitually complaining parents had a basis for their dissatisfaction and mistrust. The second fold proactively initiated preparation for the on-site monitoring by the state for which the district was long overdue. District leadership, understandably, had a driving interest in entering every program, ameliorating weaknesses and building upon documented strengths.

The process was spearheaded through designated chairpersons recruited from current faculty. Resulting findings were incorporated into an action plan, including timelines, and were presented to campus and district committees, campus and district administration, and the local board of education. The process, action plan, and accompanying timeline were updated annually. I continued year after year to be at the helm. Through this intensive internal system and other factors the district progressed from a state accountability rating of acceptable to a state accountability rating of exemplary. The vanguard of the accountability system was in my court—through the on-site monitoring system, through my office.

As the process was implemented, some, possibly most, cheered. Others, disgruntled, were defensive and assured any who listened that it could not be done—never had been. Chairpersons assumed leadership for securing necessary documentation to determine if indeed accountable student achievement was occurring—in all subgroups—and to determine if programs were adhering to established federal, state, and local guidelines. The action plan was revised annually.

After the initial year of the system chairpersons and I were requested to lead all sessions of district professional development with the focus of each session being the in-district monitoring system, its findings, and the resulting action plan. Evaluations of sessions were extraordinary. Annually thereafter professional development included current-year monitoring findings and the status of the current-year action plan. "You have to put the paintbrush in their hand . . ." and move out of the way of the surging momentum.

Collaboration and collegiality, propelling in union toward mutually established goals, ignite a burst of energy and compassion that encompasses the environment. The foundation of collaboration, including all stakeholders, is built upon shared trust, shared goals, shared compassion, equity, shared responsibility, and shared accountability for all students in every classroom.

> This spring, when you see geese heading back north for the summer flying along in V formation, you might be interested in knowing what scientists have discovered about why they fly that way. It has been learned that as each bird flaps its wings, it creates an uplift for the bird immediately following. By flying in V formation, the whole flock adds at least 71 percent greater flying range than if each bird flew on its own.
>
> **Basic Truth #1:** *People who share a common direction and sense of community can get where they are going quicker and easier because they are traveling on the thrust of one another.*
>
> Whenever a goose falls out of formation, it suddenly feels the drag and resistance of trying to go it alone and quickly gets back into formation to take advantage of the lifting power of the bird immediately in front.

CHAPTER 4

Basic Truth #2: *If we have as much sense as a goose, we will stay in formation with those who are headed the same way we are going.*

When the lead goose gets tired, he rotates back in the wing, and another goose flies point.

Basic Truth #3: *It pays to take turns doing hard jobs—with people or with geese flying north.*

Geese honk from behind to encourage those up front to keep up their speed.

Basic Truth #4: *We need to be careful what we say when we honk from behind.*

Finally . . . when a goose becomes sick or is wounded by a gunshot and falls out, two geese fall out of formation and follow him down to help and protect him. They stay with him until he is either able to fly or until he is dead, and then they launch out on their own or with another formation to catch up with their group.

Final Truth: *If we have the sense of a goose, we will stand by each other like that.*[4]

5

BILLY

On Thursday mornings I was assigned to the elementary school. Each Thursday when I entered the building, I heard their voices—shrill, demanding, chilling. Ms. Ford was the first grade teacher, Ms. Collins the second grade teacher. They had seniority on the campus—earned from years on the front line—began their careers there—in the same building every day every week every month—twenty-eight years for Ms. Ford, thirty-two years for Ms. Collins.

The building principal was a gracious, warm, welcoming professional gentleman. If indeed he ever stepped into the front line to address the shrieking hysteria of these tyrants, it was not evident. They were there every day before he came. They would be there every day when he was gone.

Ms. Ford and Ms. Collins dehumanized their progeny for all to hear—always had, always would—self-appointed drill sergeants at the community elementary school. New hires spoke quietly, closing their doors to decrease ranting distractions. Their deafening frenzy totally corralled behavior in the cafeteria. No microphone was required. Communications of professionals, including district and campus administration, hushed in despair as the squawking of these despots escalated, the maddening intensity obliterating dialogue of any within its clutch.

- The positive school climate is student centered.
- The positive school climate is inviting.
- The positive school climate is expecting.
- The positive school climate is welcoming—every child, every parent.
- The positive school climate is accepting of differences.
- The positive school climate is encouraging.
- The positive school climate builds up—builds relationships—knows students flourish in well-cultivated, nurtured gardens of learning.
- The positive school climate celebrates the coming of each student—every day—just as he/she is.
- The positive school climate inspires the union between the teacher and the student. Together, hand in hand, they explore the unknown, searching daily the mysteries within learning, charting paths that are not yet trod, constructing building blocks of developmentally-based skills.
- The positive school climate is a learning community in which each is the learner and each is the teacher, in which students and educators reach for the other to come along for the journey.

The warmth of being enshrouded in the positive climate of a student-centered campus is readily apparent—the gentleness of greeters' voices as we enter the building, the joyous pictures on the walls of smiling children, fresh flowers at the entry, comfortable seating for guests—parents, community members, business and industry representatives. We become more relaxed. We breathe more deeply. We speak more slowly. We listen more intently. We interrupt less. We remain for lunch, helping little ones open their milk cartons, extending to the quiet child sitting alone. The students become all of our children. We volunteer. We return—again and again. We truly become partners in the education of our child—of all children. We are lifted up. We lift up.

The positive school is a deliberate choice. It is an expectation. It is planned. Students and the community are eager to enter its portals. I want to go there.

- When students step on the bus, they are genuinely greeted by the driver.
- The vehicle is in order.
- As the bus arrives on campus, staff and volunteers welcome each student by name.
- Warmth permeates the property.
- Space is well allocated, eliminating overcrowding in all locations.
- The principal is the instructional leader.
- Teachers teach.
- Staff members, present throughout the facility, represent consistency and dignity in every interaction.
- Custodians call students by name, taking pride in the glistening floors and sparkling walls.
- Maintenance personnel ensure repairs are current.
- Food service employees welcome each child as meals are distributed.
- Counselors counsel proactively.
- Students are referred to campus administration as a positive reinforcement.
- Coaches build teams of winners. Each athlete is a star.

Physicals were scheduled August 1st. Each student who planned to try out for the middle school football team was required to be present on the 1st—9:00 a.m. to 12:00 noon. It was well-known

CHAPTER 5

throughout the campus that each who tried for the team was offered a position—a team of stars. Prospective athletes were informed of the date prior to the closing of the previous school year. Parent permission forms were forwarded in June. Signed parent permissions had been returned. Reminders were mailed in July.

Doc Wharton, the local physician, scheduled the morning to complete the physicals—without cost to the district or to the parents. As a taxpayer and father of three graduates of the high school, the physicals were his local philanthropic contribution. Each of his sons received full football scholarships to prestigious universities upon graduation. "Free physicals are the least I can do to repay and support the district."

The well-plumped, silver-haired nurse, Helen, accompanied him—starched stiff in her white uniform, carrying his black medical bag, frayed and crumbling at the edges from decades of use. She knew the routine, having been his office nurse for twenty-five years—and nanny for his three boys—stethoscope, thermometer, tongue depressors, blood pressure monitor, otoscope, bandages, sterile gloves, hand sanitizer, notepad, pens (that write), sharpened pencils, flashlight.

Coaches, arriving at 7:30 a.m., anticipated an eventful morning of athletes coming and going, questions and clarifications from parents. Students commenced arriving at 7:00 a.m., restless from missed sleep the previous night, excited about events of the morning. Muscles developed during the summer were flaunted. Whiskers emerging with puberty were apparent. The athletes were electrified with expectations for a 10-0 season—for a victorious year for the middle school football team.

Physical examinations were completed about noon, Doc asking about moms and dads, brothers and sisters of athletes, patting each on the back as if he were his son. The years pass so quickly. Recalling his own sons at this fragile age, a tear flowed onto his wrinkled, veined, sagging cheek. The hormone-charged teens loitered around the field house giggling at shared moments, forecasting professional teams who would make the playoffs, marveling at teammates whose height had increased during the summer.

BILLY

Doc gathered his belongings, disrobing his white lab coat, slightly stained at the right wrist, glancing again at the virility of youth as he hobbled to his truck—left hip had been giving him some trouble lately. Helen dutifully replaced supplies in the worn medical bag, scampering to jump in as he drove away.

Coaches reviewed the reports, initiating the process of selecting the A team, the B team. Reruns of films of football games of the previous season played monotonously in the background. As one ended, the next began—one after another after another. About midafternoon each bid farewell for the evening, confident this will be the winning season for the home team. The head coach, fatigued from the rigors of the day, labored further in his office—physicals, parent permissions, equipment, schedule, team positions—checking list after list after list for readiness for the new school year.

The faint knock on the door didn't arouse him as he checked each list just one more time, rubbing his red, tired eyes. The second knock penetrated the trance. He turned toward the door, his chair squeaking on three of four bearings. "I must prepare a requisition for a new chair—so little time, so much to do before two-a-days begin." It was 4:20 in the afternoon. The disheveled figure at the door awaited his acknowledgment, wet, dripping, stringy hair, tattered clothing soaked from country sweat, propping on one leg and then the other. It was ninety-five degrees. Billy stammered. "Hi, Coach, I've come for my physical."

"Billy, physicals were completed this morning. Doc has returned to his office. Do you have any idea what time it is?" In shallow gasps Billy responded. "I don't know, Coach, it must be afternoon." "Billy, it's after 4:00." "Coach, I came as fast as I could." Billy, still standing at the door, had not yet been invited into the office. Coach reached for the glass of cold water on his desk, gulping half a glass before responding. "Billy, come in and have a seat," pointing to the one other chair in the room, hard back, salvaged from the storage room before the dump truck came. Billy entered, hesitantly, seating himself on the edge of the chair. "Billy, tell me more."

CHAPTER 5

"Well, Coach, Papa and I were riding toward school, and the car stopped right there in the road—out of gas. Papa said we don't have money to buy gas to keep driving back and forth to school so I could play with a ball, said I had chores to do so the family could eat. Coach, he was really angry. We started walking toward a house up the road, searching for help. I told Papa I'd walk on to school, that I had to be there by noon. Go on, Son. He said he'd pick me up when he found some gas. Coach, I haven't seen Papa since. Have you seen him?"

Coach knew the road well, had likely run out of gas eleven miles from the field house. Often he drove athletes home after practice. Generally, these were students whose families lived a distance from school—in shanties—poor, dirt poor. "Billy, did you walk all the way?" "No, Coach, I ran some of the time." Coach offered him a drink of cold water from the ice chest and the remainder of his bologna sandwich.

"This is Coach Brenham. May I speak with Doc Wharton?" "He's with a patient now." "I'll hold until he can speak with me." "Coach, it may be a while. We really have them stacked up here—summer flu season." Coach held for twelve minutes, awaiting the deep, deep voice of Doc. "Sure, Coach, I'll return after my last appointment. Yes, just have him stay with you. I'll be there as soon as I can."

The B team schedule for the upcoming school year was finalized months before the beginning of the season. The first game was a particularly intensive competition—playing against the long-standing rival—the community about six miles north on 287. Dads of seventh-grade athletes had donned uniforms during the last generation and had competed against dads of the opponent's team—when they were sprouting boys, yes, when they were just boys.

Parents and community members arrived early, selecting choice seats for the contest, fries and pop overflowing from their gnarled hands. Thursday night football was a community event—could see the lights all over town. All seats were occupied; community support was alive and well in this little burg. Folks in worn jeans lined

BILLY

the fences, propping on the top rail—drawling about the home team, expected plays, the rival, the memories when they ran the plays—when they were boys, sprouting boys—long ago.

"Please stand for the school song and remain standing for the pledge." Singing filled the air—off key, but filled with total allegiance to the home team. Right hands were placed over hearts for the pledge. All stood for the kickoff. Cheerleaders jumped ecstatically, legs flying in the air. "Go, team, go."

In the first quarter Billy scored the first touchdown, running seventy-two yards. The crowds cheered, jumping up and down. Applause rang throughout the stands. "Run, Billy, run." Patrons stood for the remainder of the game—would have been irreverent to sit down after that touchdown—haven't seen a play like that since I was a kid. The home team won—6 to 0—the first victory against the long-standing rival for eight years.[1]

Lawrence Kohlberg's steps of moral development guide us, the citizens of the universe, to ultimate, sacrificial, rewarding levels that culminate in behaviors that are considerate, based on individual rights, justice, dignity, and equality (Level 3). Level 1 includes personal needs and others' rules. In Level 2 judgment is based upon others' approval, expectations, values, and upon laws of society and loyalty to country. Positive school climate emulates Level 3.[2] The positive school climate is considerate, is just, is fair. Positive school climate is based upon individual rights of justice, dignity, and equality.

Step aside and as an observer peer inside the climate of your school as if you were seeing it, feeling it, sensing it, hearing it for the very first time.

- Gauge the temperature in the teachers' lounge on a scale from den of iniquity to student-centered support station. Close and lock access to this room if it strays one cat's whisker from being a student-centered support station—enough said.

CHAPTER 5

- Assess the level of welcome that parents sense when they are on campus.

  1. Is a bilingual employee assigned to the front office?
  2. Is a dedicated space with comfortable furniture reserved for parents and guests? (Local furniture stores are eager to furnish rooms for community members on campuses.)
  3. Is a pot of fresh coffee available? Is an employee assigned to maintain its freshness?
  4. Are children's books available for parents who bring preschoolers? Are developmentally-based toys available?
  5. Is a small, up-to-date library focusing on school-parent partnerships nearby for checkout by parents?
  6. Is preschool child care readily offered when parents are meeting with teachers?

- Observe dress and body language of professionals and paraprofessionals. Are dress and body language welcoming and professional? Review standards for employee appearance in district guidelines. Note employees with happy faces, with warm smiles.
- Hear the voices. Do staff members speak in definitive, positive, warm, gentle utterances? Is mutual support apparent? Does the tie of collegiality bind? Note voices of students. Listen for listening. Do adults listen to students? Do students listen to adults?
- Identify proactive school measures for health of employees. To what extent do initiatives focus on nutrition, stress reduction, weight, exercise, and other significant research-based components of health? Examine attendance records of employees, including promptness.
- Is each individual located in the most student-centered location? Are teachers teaching?

- Is the environment tidy, with flexibility for priority projects? Is space well used?
- Is each location supervised by well-trained, positive staff? Are expectations consistent?
- Are administrators client-friendly and accommodating—with students, community, parents, educators, and support personnel?
- Are students in school? Nationally the graduation rate is approximately 70 percent.[3] Students are either in school or they're not. There is not a middle ground. When students are in school, they are learning basic skills, adding to their quiver of saleable skills upon graduation.

1. Analyze student attendance.
2. Critique student discipline reports.
3. Weigh if curriculum and instructional strategies are sufficiently challenging to engage students at higher levels of Bloom's Taxonomy.[4]

Positive climate is the foundation for every effective school.

A few minutes after the tardy bell rang, a level of anxiety trickled through my body—heavier, shallow breathing, trembling hands, accelerated heartbeat, shaking voice. Tardy students entering the room chuckled, tripping over notebooks in the aisles, bumping, thumping students' desks as they ambled to their assigned location—one after another—a parade of surly, disgruntled middle school students. A substitute study hall teacher—the good news had permeated the hallway. The principal had left the building within the previous hour, driving to another campus in the district, wasn't scheduled to return for the remainder of the afternoon. It's party time.

Having recently moved to a neighboring community, I applied for substitute teaching positions as I settled into my new home. The

CHAPTER 5

telephone rang at the last minute that Tuesday morning—about 6:30. The English teacher had called in sick—doctor's appointment this morning, will return after lunch. I opened the garage door at 7:15 a.m., driving to a campus I had never seen. My schedule was handed to me when I entered the building—periods one and two eighth-grade language arts, period three study hall. "No, language arts lesson plans are not available."

Periods one and two passed rather unremarkably—implemented a typical stalling strategy. "Take three pages from your notebooks. Write a paper about one of the topics on the board. Yes, all papers will be provided for the teacher when he returns."

Study hall was located in a classroom farther down the hall on the right. Fifteen minutes after the tardy bell (shrill siren that it was) the last of the tardy students had entered the overfilled room. All desks were filled with distracted, distractible students. Few brought books for studying knowing there would be no studying today. I was losing control of the study hall. In reality, I had not been in control since the tardy bell rang—nor before. Any efforts to quiet the room were lost as whispers, then chuckles became more rambunctious, filling the room with free-flowing conversation and giggles.

If I can just make it until the dismissal bell! I watched the clock on the wall—typical round school clock, hanging askew on the peeling wall, twelve inches in diameter, minute hand progressing erratically from number to number. I was watching the second hand, psst, psst, psst, as seconds clicked. My heart was racing. My face was flush. I perspired. Five more minutes! Four minutes! Three minutes! Two minutes! One minute!

I walked to the door and opened it for the upcoming stampede—forty-five seconds, thirty seconds, fifteen seconds. Finally, the dismissal bell rang—the siren. I had survived—torn and emotionally tattered—yet survived. No gains had been made in student achievement during period three—a total loss of human potential and capacity. It was a duel, a struggle to the last second.

To this day, decades later, period three study hall on that crisp autumn morning returns in my memory. It brings me to my knees in humility for inadequacies I demonstrated on that day. Compassion for stumbling educators is embedded in my soul as a result of this experience. In every classroom someone is in control. It is either the educator or it is the student. On that given day in period three study hall thirty-five unruly, boisterous, disrespectful students were in control.

Research conducted by the National Education Association indicates one-half of teachers leave the profession within the first five years of their employment because of poor working conditions and low salaries. Teachers leaving the profession and entering other employment areas have been ongoing concerns in the nation for decades. Those with master's degrees have increased from 23 percent to 50 percent since the 1960s, yet the revolving door of educated professionals entering and leaving teaching positions swings rapidly, depriving educational institutions of quality professionals.[5]

Poor working conditions! Success characteristics of the WOW school, the school with the positive climate, as enumerated by Phillip Schlechty, *Working on the Work*, include, but are not limited to, the following:

- The effective school is a way of life. It is an internal system.
- The effective school introduces students to the culture in which they will function and provides skills and tools for success.
- The effective school is led by a trusted, effective leader.
- The effective school flourishes in an environment of collegiality.

CHAPTER 5

- The effective school provides students engaging work—every day—every day.[6]

When success characteristics of effective schools permeate the instructional environment, working conditions illuminate authentic involvement and achievement by all. Students, parents, community members, and educators are eager to cross the threshold—every day. Stakeholders reach deeply for all children, lifting every child to higher levels of functioning—academically, socially, and emotionally.

6

RED, YELLOW, BLACK, AND WHITE (AND BROWN?)!

It was in 1902 that Martha Atee, age two, boarded a ship at the port in Beirut, Syria, with Gito and Gita for the unpredictable, treacherous voyage to the land of the free—America. The three—Martha, Gito, and Gita—carried their earth's possessions in assorted luggage—one tattered bag per person, donated by family members, shepherds in the desert land.

The creaking ship, instead, landed on the coast of eastern Mexico, the restless, hungry passengers stepping onto shore after weeks of rolling with the waves on the vast ocean. Moving inland, Gito and Gita struggled daily for their survival and for the survival of their precious little girl, Martha. In time they settled in Monterrey, selling wares for sustenance in the marketplace and on the street corners. Through the influence of her parents Martha spoke Syrian fluently. As her brief childhood years passed, she communicated equally well in Spanish.

Nahum Kalil Tipshrani, born in 1886, likewise embarked on a seafaring journey from Beirut to the free world at the tender, impressionable age of twelve. He departed Syria as Nahum Kalil Tipshrani. He emerged from Ellis Island as Nahum Kalil, never again reclaiming his Mediterranean surname.

CHAPTER 6

Nahum, his mother, and two brothers, alone in a foreign land, relocated through the years from New York Harbor into the interior of the United States. On city streets the boys hawked homemade bread and other delicacies baked daily by my great-grandmother—a hand-to-mouth existence. Nahum and his mother settled in Texas. A brother traveled west into Arizona. The third son immigrated farther south into Brazil.

Nahum was fourteen years the senior of Martha; however, following traditions of the old country Gito and Gita betrothed Martha to Nahum. Nahum was twenty-eight; Martha was at the tender age of fourteen.

At the age of fifteen Martha gave birth to her first child—a girl baby. At the age of sixteen Martha gave birth to her second child—a girl baby. At the age of eighteen Martha gave birth to her third child—a girl baby. At the age of twenty Martha gave birth to her fourth child—a boy baby. At the age of twenty-one Martha gave birth to her fifth child—a girl baby.

The fifth baby child of Martha and Nahum Kalil is my mother. They parented eleven children, eking a meager livelihood selling tomatoes, lettuce, onions, beans, other vegetables, and fruit on wooden tables in the farmer's market—before the Great Depression, during the Great Depression, and after the Great Depression. Until their deaths three languages were spoken in the household—Syrian (developing into Lebanese), Spanish, broken English.

Red, yellow, black, and white (and brown?)! I celebrate my heritage. Every child has a life story. Every educator has a legacy, also. It is embedded deep within our inner beings.

During the last days of Granny Kalil, I moved my chair closer to her, eager to capture her penetrating truisms. "Granny, you are the mother of eleven, each loving you immeasurably. The spouse of every child loves and cares for you as their mother." She focused her eyes on mine, speaking softly. "They're all my children. They're all my children."

RED, YELLOW, BLACK, AND WHITE (AND BROWN?)!

The kaleidoscope of learners in public schools in this nation reaches for educators who understand and live "they're all my children." Effective educators touch children just as they are, gathering this rainbow of learners into the fold. Effective educators unabashedly claim ownership for the present and future well-being and success of each student. Effective educators are the foundation for educational reform in institutions throughout this nation—the momentum vibrating from ethereal skyscrapers through farmland of small boroughs, from East Coast to West, from mountaintops to border ghettoes. The beat resonates, quivering through the land.

> I woke up this morning. What did I see way up in the sky? I saw a pretty rainbow smiling down at me higher than the birds can fly.[1]

Approximately 336 languages are spoken or signed in the United States.[2] Some 145 languages are spoken in New York City schools.[3] About 112 languages are spoken in homes in the San Francisco metropolitan area.[4] By 2020 approximately two-thirds of students enrolled in schools in this nation will be African American, Asian, Hispanic, or Native American. Many will be children of first-generation immigrants.[5]

Identify the dazzling array of languages spoken in your home community, your district, your campus, your classroom—the rainbow of diversity through which the proverbial pot of gold is the prize. The glittering prize that schools that work eagerly open at the end of the rainbow is an educated citizenry, a citizenry well equipped for the rigors of the twenty-first century.

Effective educators assess their strategic, pivotal position in the success of the brilliant colors of this rainbow of humanity. Am I a stumbling block, or am I a stepping-stone? Am I a villain, or am I a saint? The ball of hope and high expectations for all children—red, yellow, black, and white (and brown?)!—is tossed to every educator. The bleachers are filled to capacity with anticipating

CHAPTER 6

stakeholders awaiting my next play. The crowd peers as I position and reposition on the field. Time is critical. Minutes, then seconds, on the scoreboard are clicking—nineteen, eighteen, seventeen . . . Every day, every second, as an educator, the ball of hope and high expectations is tossed to me—to me. Do I . . .

- eagerly anticipate the arrival of each student on the first day of school?
- contact every parent *prior* to the beginning of the school year, assuring each I cherish their providing their dearest treasure to me for safekeeping, development, and fulfillment?
- have my house in order prior to the first day? My classroom is efficiently organized—so routines are unremarkable, so learning is remarkable.
- practice, practice, practice procedures during the first week (and after holidays), knowing a secure learning environment contributes to student achievement the remainder of the year?
- provide procedural and behavioral expectations for parents?
- welcome and encourage student-centered volunteer opportunities from parents and from others?
- greet every student by name as each enters the classroom?
- model behavioral expectations? Am I courteous? punctual? organized? prepared?
- begin parent conferences with definitive strengths of their child prior to discussing areas of concern?
- listen?
- capture each moment for instruction—each—as a treasured moment in time that will never come again? Am I focused?
- distribute classroom leadership opportunities among students equitably (greeting visitors, position in cafeteria/library line) so each may be a brightly illuminated star?

- nondiscriminately assign responsibilities in cooperative learning groups and peer tutoring? Through my influence and expectations, is a support system of compassion and fairness apparent among all students?
- invite family members (parents, grandparents, aunts, uncles) to sing songs in native clothing—tell stories of treasured times—prepare meals from the old country? Are holidays from representative ethnicities and nationalities included on my class calendar?
- select textbooks and additional instructional materials that reflect international peoples, customs, monetary systems, traditions?
- distribute questions among all students? Do I pause sufficiently as each builds a response based upon knowledge, confidence, and dignity?

Multiculturalism presents itself through a myriad of faces—red, yellow, black, and white (and brown?)! From the first day of school of any school year to the last the rainbow of diversity infiltrates every classroom. I see their expecting, fragile faces even now.

- Jared appeared at the door—a small-sized, ninth-grade male, downcast eyes, abrupt movements, snarled lips. Upon my greeting and welcoming him, he stumbled to his desk, hunkering down with a loud thump, slouching to near lying position, flat affect. His father, a guard at the local prison, left him days ago at the security gate—promising to return for him. Neighbors took him in—no father in sight. Weeks later Mama came for Jared. He never returned to the district.
- Darlene was a female of slight build—appeared malnourished, probably was. I don't recall seeing her hair combed.

CHAPTER 6

I don't recall seeing her smile. "Don't recall" is a lengthy expanse of time. I interacted with her for five years—before she was enrolled in my classroom, when she was enrolled in my classroom, after she was enrolled in my classroom.

Her peers taunted her. The more they taunted, the more Darlene withdrew—day after day after day. I was a novice teacher then; I had few arrows in my quiver.

I failed her. She came to me sobbing with her emotional pains. I listened. She cried. The bell rang. "Students, pass your homework to the front of the row. Open your textbooks to page 279."

As I reflect on Darlene, I grieve. If I would have touched her wounds, together we could have charted a path for her of dignity, of respect. I shudder to consider the wasted life she may be living. Wastedness in one individual is wastedness for society—to consider what might have been—for one, for all.

- Robert was a big-built, ninth-grade student—the size of an adult male—resulting from retention one or more times during earlier years. He hated school. He hated me. Every day—every day since the first day—he defiantly approached the principal demanding to be reassigned from my class. Every day the principal declined. Every day Robert sauntered slovenly to class—slamming the door, grumbling in a muttered growl. Every day he fell in his chair, muttering, chin on chest, arms folded.

As the year progressed, Robert's attitude and behavior turned full circle. He evidently learned to enjoy the course, becoming actively engaged, developing a self-appointed leadership role—first to arrive, last to leave. In time he became my guardian—lifting here, moving there, commandeering any task he could see—or imagine. With skills he was developing and the apparent attitude change, I had great expectations for Robert becoming a staunch citizen of the community.

In tenth grade I heard of him, or from him, occasionally—not often. In eleventh grade I heard of him, or from him—not at all. It was two years later on a muggy, sweltering summer afternoon I opened the daily newspaper. Scanning the various headings, my eyes darted rapidly from topic to topic. I glanced hastily at Crime & Punishment. I wouldn't know anyone listed in this section.

His name catapulted from the newspaper print—Robert—*breaking and entering*—a tragic, tragic loss for Robert, a tragic loss for me, a tragic loss for society. Children who live their childhood in poverty are twice as likely to be retained and/or drop out of school. Approximately 50 percent of all African American children are poor.[6] Robert lived his childhood in poverty. Robert is African American.

- Tammy was a pretty girl, yet pale, acne erupting here and there on her porcelain complexion—no smiles—very, very quiet. Her quietness was so pervasive that neither her presence nor her absence was remarkable. She struggled with reading—struggling quietly.

Tammy was absent frequently. Generally, when she wasn't absent, she was tardy—an academically lost eighth-grade student in a strange land—every day. Consequently, when she was tardy the day of the campus alert, I was totally nonsuspecting. The secret code announcement screeched through the worn, outdated speaker system informing all of the drill. Faculty knew the code. The school had received an anonymous telephone call that a bomb was planted in the building.

Law enforcement officials swarmed on to the property, marching in from all directions, flashing lights—strobelike—atop vehicles. Methodically and swiftly the students were

CHAPTER 6

guided outdoors. Maintain control. Form a straight line. My classroom was on the second floor. We were the last group to exit the building.

The school was searched—from bow to stern—each student's locker opened, closed, opened, closed, opened, closed. The clanging could be heard by the restless students. No bomb was located. After forty-five minutes of lost instructional time, classes were released to enter the building.

Within ten minutes the building principal appeared at my door and informed me the call had been traced to Tammy's telephone. He instructed me to nonremarkably reenter my classroom and encourage Tammy to come with me into the hall (while the other perplexed students watched on). Quietly, quietly, quietly Tammy came with me. Tammy was so compliant. She willingly, quietly, followed my requests every day, no questions asked. Today was no different.

She and I walked side by side out of the classroom, her head down, no eye contact. The principal and law enforcement officials were waiting in the hall. Despondently, compliantly, she walked with them down the hall, down the stairs. I now can see Tammy walking away from me, shuffling—quietly—tattered and torn, downcast.

I never saw Tammy again. For each of us—and from all citizens of this nation—"Roll of thunder, hear my cry!"[7]

Diversity of students entering thresholds of public schools is as varied as a patchwork quilt. It is crucial and urgent for educators to peer into this kaleidoscope of learners and acknowledge the vast numbers of students exiting portals of local schools daily prior to graduation, never to return again. Every school day in America more than 2,000 high school students drop out of school.[8] Poverty indeed may be a factor in these sobering numbers.

RED, YELLOW, BLACK, AND WHITE (AND BROWN?)!

Poverty is the gut-wrenching survival mode in which multitudes of students live. Recipients of Women, Infants, and Children (WIC) increased by 65 percent from 1992–2006. WIC is a federally funded program providing low-income women and their families assistance in obtaining food and other types of support.[9]

Research conducted by Renzulli and Park reveals 15 to 25 percent of gifted students nationwide leave school before graduation.[10] Many gifted students who drop out of school are from low-income families and racial minority groups, their parents having achieved "low levels of education."[11]

The teacher is the lighthouse that guides students from depths of poverty safely to the shore of hope and high expectations through which they may build fulfilling lives. A fulfilling life enriches the individual. It, additionally, enriches the social and taxpaying structure of the community, state, and nation.

> It was Ms. Lawrence. Ms. Lawrence was my 3rd grade teacher. I learned to read in 3rd grade.
>
> We were poor—clean-to-the-bone poor. With the approach of winter, Mother and Dad hammered sides of cardboard boxes onto walls of our shanty, blocking shivering arctic air from blowing through the cracks.
>
> School was not a priority. As Mother and Dad distributed the meager income from cattle sales and from cotton picked in the fields, no money was set aside for school supplies.
>
> Ms. Lawrence didn't laugh at me. She didn't laugh at me when I completed my homework on torn grocery bags.[12]

It was Ms. Lawrence. This poverty-stricken third-grade student from the back roads of print deprivation and academic apathy entered college following high school graduation, successfully completing the doctorate degree. It was Ms. Lawrence.

CHAPTER 6

Failure to help the gifted child reach his potential is a societal tragedy, the extent of which is difficult to measure, but which is surely great. How can we measure the sonata unwritten, the curative drug undiscovered, the absence of political insight? They are the difference between what we are and what we could be as a society.

—James J. Gallagher (as cited in National Education Association)[13]

Seeds of fairness are conceived early—early in our development. "Red, Yellow, Black and White" is a song from my childhood that depicts various nationalities. "(and Brown?)!" is added to the title and penetrating message of this chapter. The years of my childhood in which I gleefully sang this song I lived thirty miles north of the Rio Grande, thirty miles north of the barrios of Matamoras, Mexico. Ethnicities included in these childhood verses did not include one of the ethnicities of my childhood peers—(and Brown?)!—peers who sat next to me day after day after day in my classrooms. Thorns borne from such inequality prick the memories of all participants—including the memories of educators.

Jennifer Thompson-Cannino and Ronald Cotton poignantly tell their heart-wrenching story of injustice. Thompson-Cannino in error identified Cotton as the perpetrator of crime against her. Through this misjudgment and injustice, Cotton lived eleven years of his life behind bars paying for a crime he did not commit. Cotton is African American. Thompson-Cannino is white.[14]

Educators grieve and deride such unfairness—failing to look at the reflection in the mirror. May it be that countless prejudgments in halls and classrooms of educational institutions across this nation have negatively altered lives of children—forever? Prejudgment against children, the wounds of which crust into scars in adulthood, "is a societal tragedy...", is "the difference between what we are and what we could be as a society."

RED, YELLOW, BLACK, AND WHITE (AND BROWN?)!

Envision a learning community of acceptance and encouragement, a community that is uplifting for all stakeholders in the schoolhouse—educator to educator—educator to student—student to educator—student to student—the orchestra chamber of learning. The teacher, the conductor, is the maestro.

He stands, arms opened, before the musicians—the students. Practice is unrelenting; it is every day. The waltz commences—the woodwinds, the brass, the percussion, the strings, each executing perfection of the whole, the excellence of each individual. And the dance begins. The audience hushes as the melody encapsulates the chamber, rushing to their feet with the last chord. The maestro bows in humility, motioning for all—yes, all—members of the orchestra to stand in unison—Red, Yellow, Black, and White (and Brown?)!—poor, wealthy, pretty, homely, gifted, disabled, revered, neglected, bathed squeaky clean, unkempt and dirty—all students.

> We are responsible for children. . .
>> who erase holes in their math workbooks . . .
>> who never "counted potatoes" . . .
> We are responsible for children . . .
>> who bring us sticky kisses and fistfuls of dandelions . . .
>> who hug us in a hurry, who forget their lunch money . . .
>> who . . . sing off-key . . .
> We are responsible for those . . .
>> who never get dessert . . .
>> who have no safe blanket to drag behind them . . .
>> who don't have rooms to clean . . .
>> whose pictures aren't on anybody's dresser . . .
>> whose monsters are real . . .
> We are responsible for children . . .
>> who spend their allowance before Tuesday . . .
>> who have visits from the tooth fairy . . .
>> whose tears sometimes make us laugh and whose smiles make us cry . . .

CHAPTER 6

We are responsible for those . . .
    whose nightmares come in the daytime . . .
    who will eat anything . . .
    who have never seen a dentist . . .
    who aren't spoiled by anybody . . .
    who go to bed hungry and cry themselves to sleep . . .
    who live and move, but have no being . . .
We are responsible for children . . .[15]

7

THE Y IN THE ROAD

Effective educators begin with the end, the destination, in mind. The destination of educational institutions—the goal—is an educated, responsible, contributing citizenry through adulthood. The age of majority commences at age eighteen. The age of majority designates adulthood. Calculating a life span of eighty years, adulthood comprises approximately 79 percent of one's life span.

To what extent have I prepared my students for adulthood—approximately 79 percent of their lives? Am I the saint, or am I the villain? Covey charges effective individuals to begin with the end, the destination, in mind.[1]

We have come to the Y in the road. Identify, qualitatively and quantitatively, the end in mind. The end, the destination, determines the road we travel. Consider decisions that are made daily. Does my instruction build bridges between learning activities and the workplace—real-life applications? Do learning activities generalize from school to adulthood?

Look in the mirror—again. May this moment be the first moment in which I, an educator, have internalized the reality that the majority of the life span in which my students will live is

Table 7.1. Life Span: Birth through Age Eighty

Birth	→Age 4	→5% of life span
Kindergarten	→Grade 5	→7.5% of life span
Grade 6	→Grade 8	→3.75% of life span
Grade 9	→Grade 12	→5% of life span
AGES 18	→80	→78.75% OF LIFE SPAN!

adulthood? Am I preparing those in my tutelage—for a life—for a world—about which we do not yet clearly know—a world we may now only see faintly?

Am I the carpenter who constructs a foundation of skills upon which my students will flourish for approximately 79 percent of their lives? Or am I shuddering with regret at the false promises, low expectations, wasted time that are lost forever—lost forever in the lives of children, never to be regained?

Ineffective teachers lay brick. Effective teachers build strong walls of brick to dissuade raging storms of life. Exemplary teachers erect cathedrals of humanity—edifices toward which all may reach and enter for immeasurable fulfillment and productivity through life's journey.[2]

Which teacher am I?

Twenty-first-century graduates are by birth natives of the universe—global citizens in an internationally competitive marketplace. Examine cutting-edge skills critically vital for the twenty-first-century economy. The twenty-first-century worker . . .

- is a lifelong learner.
- embraces change.
- is an effective communicator.
- is a critical, analytical thinker.
- approaches challenges creatively.
- is self-directed, self-regulated.
- is a positive team member.

- celebrates the unknown, the mysteries not yet understood.
- is well versed in innovative worldwide technology applications.

Effective education that meets needs for the twenty-first-century workplace exceeds demands of this decade and the next, exceeds demands of this generation and the next. Decisions made today—best-laid plans of the committed—traverse the twenty-first century into the twenty-second—and beyond. Revolutionary change propels at an unprecedented pace—fueled through unlimited, nanosecond technology. Goals established in this decade, strategies implemented in this century blaze the trail for citizens of this planet infinitely through time.

Contemplate your role in this revolution. Are you a vibrant, integral member of the solution team? Are your skills, your energies sharper today than they were yesterday, than they were last week, than they were last month, last year? For those whose passion within your soul is to be a trailblazer for children, then run along beside the throng of vigorous stakeholders shouldering the torch of excellence in education.

If your steps are weary—if you cannot feel the zeal—if the torch of excellence is flickering in your vision—then step aside. Educators—from the classroom to the central office—worthy of this journey—educators who embrace the opportunity of impacting students in this nation's schools—are those who are invigorated by the brilliance of an educated citizenry. Educators who have faltered—who cannot feel the fervor—who cannot envision the torch of excellence in twenty-first-century education—*are in need of removal from classrooms, campuses, and districts in this country.*

Stand back. As an observer, peer into classrooms in this nation. Is the curriculum relevant to meet needs of each student—each student—and meet needs of society as a whole today—and in the future? Either it is, or it is not. Are schools functioning at a higher

CHAPTER 7

level of expectations today than they were last year, in the last decade, in the last century? Either they are, or they are not. Momentum for positive change inherently moves forward. Evaluate this momentum in educational institutions—positive change on behalf of students—positive change on behalf of civilization.

Every twenty-six seconds a high school student in the United States drops out of school. The short-term and long-term implications are heartbreaking and wasteful—lower-paying unreliable employment, malnutrition, poor health, increased rates of incarceration. The sobering results are incalculable. Dropout rates penetrate deeper among minority students. Approximately 50 percent of African American students and Hispanic students enrolled in public schools nationwide do not complete school.[3]

Economic loss for society as a result of nationwide dropout figures is immeasurable in lost wages, lost taxes, lost productivity. Business and industry, the hub of the national and international economic structure, are recipients of a graduated—or a nongraduated—workforce. This workforce is either well prepared—or ill prepared—for rigors of the twenty-first-century workplace. Inadequately prepared employees perpetuate an already struggling national economy in the competitive international marketplace.

Spotlight a young student in your school. Calculate skills he/she must master in approximately a dozen years of education to be well equipped for postsecondary education and/or the workplace. Lay aside the inertia of "yes, but" and acknowledge today, this moment, the greatest causal factor for student learning in the schoolhouse is the educator—from the classroom to the central office.

With deliberate urgency evaluate the total curriculum of your school for relevance for the twenty-first century. A relevant curriculum challenges students. A relevant curriculum encourages students, boys and girls, to return to school day after day, semester after semester, year after year. Begin on the home front—the classroom. The classroom is the arena in which the flame of revolutionary change ignites schools locally, nationally, and internationally. Progress from the classroom to the campus to the district.

- Is a vertical curricular continuum of real-life experiences developed for students of all ages from prekindergarten through grade twelve?
- Is the continuum developed upon a longitudinal progression from career awareness to career exploration to career preparation?
- Is the continuum built upon current labor market projections and needs?
- Are instructional strategies through all grade levels immersed in . . .
  1. analysis, synthesis, and evaluation levels of Bloom's Taxonomy?
  2. dialogue with representatives from business, industry, agencies, and elected officials?
  3. one-to-one sessions with adult mentors?
  4. job shadowing in a variety of work settings?
  5. field trips to businesses of local employers/postsecondary education institutions?
  6. real-life experiences in the community?
- Is the faculty knowledgable about current labor market projections, needs, and resources?
- Does annual professional development target short-term and long-term labor market projections?
- Is development of an educated citizenry—the end in mind—within the mission statement of the district and of each campus and within subsequent action plans?
- Are definitive accountability measures in place for every educator to well prepare graduates to compete globally in

CHAPTER 7

an international economy and to lead in the twenty-first century?
- Are community/business/agency/postsecondary education representatives on each advisory council?
- Are agreements with postsecondary education activated for designated high school students to simultaneously earn high school and college credits?
- Is enrichment/advanced placement offered at every grade level for students to pursue identified areas of interest and ability?

The most critical need in public education in this century is to elevate schools to meet needs and demands of a global economy. Rigorous, synergetic, innovative, current, ever-changing curriculum is the vehicle to elevate twenty-first-century classrooms into vivid, living think tanks that electrify curiosities of students—and educators.

The Y in the road is here. The Y in the road is now—today. The risk involved in revolutionizing every classroom in America is urgent, is a necessity for students, for the nation, for the planet. Complacency by maintaining inadequate, unchallenging, outdated educational models is a far greater risk for this civilization and for civilizations to come.

> For schools to serve their purposes, they must be organized around students and the needs students bring with them to school, and they must provide students with work (experiences) that responds to these needs . . . ensuring . . . every child, every day, is provided with engaging work . . . that results in . . . learning . . . that is important to the child and to the continuation of the culture.[4]

8

TEDDY

Our challenge is to mobilize the knowledge we have in the service of ends that we can justify . . . to follow principles even when they go against our self-interest, to take the risk of speaking out when we see injustices occurring, and . . . to create or join institutions that reflect our higher selves, our better selves.[1]

- Are high school graduates better prepared in this century for a productive, fulfilling adulthood than they were in the last?
- Are instructional strategies in classrooms in this nation based upon razor-sharp findings from twenty-first-century research?
- *Are teachers aware* of twenty-first-century, razor-sharp findings?
- Is current research and its applicability within every—yes, every—professional development scheduled by the school?
- Whose responsibility is it to throw this ball, to hit this pitch?

The truth as it is may not be as we wish it to be. It is a new day, however. Educators have another time at bat. The brilliance

CHAPTER 8

of high expectations for every child may be out of your sight now—the brilliance upon which you based your selection of the profession of education. However, "it's morning again in America."[2] It's morning again, hand in hand, with fellow citizens worldwide.

> Understanding global forces that impinge upon our daily lives should be one of the central competencies that all individuals have to participate as effective citizens in local, national, and transnational communities. The development of a cross-cultural empathetic consciousness and the capacities to work on behalf of international human rights and environmental preservations should be overriding priorities for education systems everywhere.[3]

High school graduates enter postsecondary education and the workforce prepared for inherent challenges therein when educators *know and practice* twenty-first-century skills every day in classrooms in this nation—every day. Teachers most likely to succeed in reaching each child, in equipping every child for productive adulthood . . .

- exude a bedrock belief that children are not defined nor doomed by their life circumstances,
- believe students are teachable even when they are not lovable,
- bring steely determination to reach children, refusing to blame their own lack of success on the students, parents, or the neighborhoods,
- bear primary responsibility for sparking their students' desire to learn,
- know success results from persistence and effort,
- expect students to have great potential,
- assume responsibility for doing more,
- never stop trying.[4]

TEDDY

From the first day he stepped into my classroom, I disliked Teddy. Teachers (although everyone knows differently) do not have favorites, but most especially they are not to show dislike for a child, not any child. Nevertheless, every year there is one, possibly two, to which one becomes attached.

Teachers are human; it's human nature to like handsome, intelligent people. Sometimes there is one student, or two, toward whom the teacher just doesn't relate. I had considered, however, myself quite capable of handling my personal feelings—until Teddy walked into my life.

There wasn't a child I particularly liked that year, but Teddy was most assuredly one I disliked. He was dirty, not just occasionally, but every day. His hair hung low over his ears; he held it out of his eyes as he wrote his assignments. He had a peculiar odor which I could not identify. By the end of the first week he was hopelessly behind. Not only was he behind, he was slow. I withdrew from him immediately.

Any teacher will tell you it's more of a pleasure to teach a bright child. It's definitely more rewarding for one's ego. Any teacher worth her credentials can channel work to the bright child, keeping him challenged and learning, while she places her major effort on the slower ones. Any teacher can do this. Most teachers do it, but I didn't—not that year. I concentrated on my best students; the others could follow along as well as they could. I took pleasure in using my red pen when I marked Teddy's papers. "Poor work," I wrote with a flourish.

I did not ridicule Teddy, although my attitude was apparent to the class. He quickly became the class "goat," the outcast, the unlovable, the unloved. He knew I didn't like him, but he didn't know why. Nor did I know why I felt such an intense dislike for him. He was a little boy no one cared about; I made no effort in his behalf.

Fall Festival and Thanksgiving holidays came and went; I marked happily with my red pen. As Christmas holidays approached, I knew Teddy could not be promoted to sixth grade. He would be a repeater. To justify my expectations, I opened his

CHAPTER 8

cumulative folder. He had low grades for the first four years, but no grade failure. How he had made it, I didn't know. I closed my mind to the personal remarks.

First Grade: Teddy shows promise by work and attitude, but has a poor home situation.

Second Grade: Mother is terminally ill. He receives little help at home.

Third Grade: Teddy is a pleasant boy, helpful, but too serious, slow learner. Mother passed away at the end of the school year.

Fourth Grade: Very slow, but well-behaved. Father shows no interest.

They passed him four times; he will certainly repeat fifth grade. "Do him good," I said to myself.

Paper and popcorn chains encircled the little tree on the reading table. Gifts were heaped underneath, waiting for the big moment. It was the last day before Christmas holidays. Teachers typically receive several gifts at Christmas; my gifts that year seemed more plentiful than other years. Every student brought me one. Each unwrapping brought squeals of delight; the proud giver received effusive "thank yous."

Teddy's gift wasn't the last one I picked up; it was in the middle of the pile. Its wrapping was a brown paper bag; Christmas trees and red balls were colored all over it. It was stuck together with masking tape. "For Miss Thompson, from Teddy" was written. The class was silent. I felt conspicuous, embarrassed as they watched me unwrap the gift.

Two items fell to my desk—a gaudy rhinestone bracelet with several stones missing and a small bottle of dime store cologne, half empty. I could hear the snickers and whispers. "Isn't this lovely?" I asked, placing the bracelet on my wrist. "Teddy, would you help me fasten it?" He smiled shyly as he closed the clasp and as I held my wrist for all to admire. There were a few hesitant "oohs and ahhs." As I dabbed the cologne behind my ears, the little girls lined up for a dab behind their ears.

After we finished opening gifts and after refreshments, the bell rang. The children one by one exclaimed "See you next year!" and

"Merry Christmas!" But Teddy waited at his desk until all were gone. He walked toward me. "You smell just like Mom," he said softly. "Her bracelet looks real pretty on you, too. I'm glad you like it." He left quickly. I locked the door, returned to my desk, and wept, resolving to make up to Teddy what I had deliberately deprived him of—a teacher who cared.

I stayed every afternoon with Teddy from the first day of school after Christmas holidays until the last day of the school year. Sometimes we worked together. Sometimes he worked alone while I prepared lesson plans or graded papers. Gradually there was a definite upward curve in his grades.

He did not repeat fifth grade. His final averages were among the highest in the class. Although I learned he would be moving out of state when the school year ended, I was not worried for him. Teddy had reached a level of success and confidence that would be with him wherever he lived. As we were taught in teacher certification courses, "Success builds success."

I had received no communication from Teddy for seven years when the first letter arrived. "Dear Miss Thompson, I want you to be the first to know I will be graduating second in my class next month. Very truly yours, Teddy Stallard." I sent him a card of congratulations and a pen and pencil set, wondering what his plans were after graduation.

Four years later, the second letter arrived. "Dear Miss Thompson, I want you to be the first to know I will be graduating first in my class. The university has not been easy. Very truly yours, Teddy Stallard." I sent him a pair of sterling monogrammed cuff links and a card, so proud of him I could burst.

Today Teddy's third letter arrived. "Dear Miss Thompson, I want you to be the first to know as of today I am Theodore J. Stallard, MD. How about that? I'm going to be married in July, the 27th. I want you to come to the wedding and sit where Mom would if she were here. I'll have no family present. Dad died last year. Very truly yours, Ted Stallard."

I smiled as I read the words, my heart swelled with a pride I had no right to feel. I had not seen Teddy since he was a student in my

CHAPTER 8

fifth-grade class fifteen years ago. I placed, one by one, his letters in my cedar chest with my other cherished items. "Dear Ted, Congratulations! You made it. I'll be at your wedding with bells on."[5]

Who is Teddy? Describe him—grooming, posture, affect. Is he enrolled on my campus—in my classroom? Is he welcome? Is he welcomed?

As an educator you will make a difference in the life of every child—either positive or negative—every child. Look in the mirror again. Analyze the difference you will make. Every educator has the opportunity to bring in the home run of high expectations for each child. Learning that occurs in classrooms across America is a reflection of teaching—day after day after day—that is executed in those rooms. It is the teacher who makes the difference—positive or negative. It is the teacher.

Every student has gifts, has talents, has strengths. Teachers have the capacity to illuminate the light of these gifts, of these talents, of these strengths. Gifts, talents, strengths may lay hidden, later to shine, hidden from years of potential productivity—a vast wasteland.

- Isaac Newton was a low achiever in elementary school.
- Beethoven's talents in music were overlooked, ridiculed by his music teacher.
- Teachers of Thomas Edison believed he had below-average intelligence.
- Wernher von Braun, rocket physicist, scored below passing in ninth-grade algebra.
- Louis Pasteur was rated as "mediocre" in chemistry at Royal College.
- Fred Waring was refused participation in high school chorus.
- Winston Churchill repeated sixth grade.
- Leo Tolstoy flunked out of college.[6]

TEDDY

Effective teachers expect differences, nurture differences, celebrate differences. Talents—gifts—may not be apparent when students bring characteristics—differences—to the classroom that mask hidden potential.

I sat across from his desk. I had always admired him—a seasoned educator in his fifties, a building principal, student centered, soft-spoken, deliberate in his thought processing, beginning to discuss retirement, looking back through the years—difficult, difficult years. "I was the thirteenth of fourteen children," he initiated one day, "poor, dirt poor, picked cotton as soon as I could drag the sack. I'm one of two in the family to finish high school. I'm not sure Dad had any formal education. Mother didn't finish high school—married at fourteen—first child at fifteen."

"I failed every class in eighth grade except PE and Vo Ag. I repeated the grade, struggled to pass each course." I listened in awe, silent, tasting every morsel of the pain, the lifetime of stress. "I dropped out of school in tenth grade—overage, clumsy, socially awkward, continually failing. I signed up for the military, finished my GED. I continue to have difficulty reading. I read very, very slowly—one word at a time, trying to understand the meaning."

"Upon my discharge I enrolled in college, paying with the GI Bill, recorded all the lectures. Professors granted my requests for extended time to complete tests, oral administration of exams. I graduated with a bachelor's degree in education, then a master's degree. I've completed all course requirements for the doctorate degree. I can't go any farther. I don't have the reading and writing skills to conduct the research and write the dissertation."

"I've always felt like I missed something. I chose a career in education. Maybe I can guide students for whom the journey is so very difficult, as it has been for me."[7] The deafening silence in his office as he concluded enveloped the room.

CHAPTER 8

Describe the message you send to children daily. Do you search for greatness in each student? Every child has greatness. Do you extend the hand of learning together, to come along with me? Every teacher is a student. Every student is a teacher. Do you explore with students at the beginning of the school year their strengths through assessments of brain dominance, learning styles, multiple intelligences? Do you teach through their strengths? Or do you habitually, day after day, year after year, teach through *your* strengths, knowing their growth and dignity are compromised through this travesty?

It was my conference period. He entered my classroom—a gentle giant, a professional gentleman—my supervisor. He looked toward the chalkboard. He knew this school well. He was an elementary student here during his childhood. "Was it that important I copied every word every day? My mathematics teacher wrote prolifically on the board. I could look as she wrote and solve the problems in my head, but we were instructed to transfer the information onto our papers."

"I printed very slowly. It was particularly difficult for me to copy from the board. Letter by letter, word by word, problems were laboriously transferred to my paper. Comprehension was lost in the process. To this day I print slowly when transferring information from a wallboard to my paper."

"Only those students who copied all the problems from the chalkboard to our papers could play outside during recess. I was alone in my classroom during many, many recesses in elementary school—copying information from the chalkboard to my paper." He paused; he stammered. "Was it that important I copied every problem every day—every day?"[8]

Doldrums of years, of decades, of ineffective educational strategies can now be locked in sealed vaults, never to reoccur again in this nation's schools. It's morning again in America. Educators have another time at bat.

- Are biographies, snapshots of adults who have achieved success in the face of adversity, embedded horizontally and vertically in schoolwide curriculum?
- Is the child in the wheelchair inspired by a president who led this nation through World War II—from a wheelchair?
- Has the young African American boy been profoundly impacted by the incalculable influence that is before us every day—a president from a minority ethnicity?
- Is the Hispanic female invigorated with the appointment of a Hispanic female to the Supreme Court of this land?
- Are children from poverty enshrouded and emblazoned by example after example of those who have broken chains of poverty and elevated themselves into affluence and leadership positions during adult years (i.e., Ronald Wilson Reagan, William Jefferson Clinton, Abraham Lincoln)?
- Are professions illuminated that may be outside of the academia of reading/language arts, mathematics, social studies, sciences (i.e., the arts, the theater, the opera, the orchestra)?

To reach children it may be necessary to kneel—to touch the wounds of who they are, of where they've been, of what they know and have experienced. Children enter school doors every day just as they are. We can kneel. We can lift them up gently, to heights beyond their current awareness, yet, most assuredly, to heights within their grasp, awaiting their reaching. We can strive, can struggle with each child. In so doing each is the student; each is the teacher.

Relevance and accessibility to cutting-edge twenty-first-century learning are inherent necessities in educational institutions in this nation. Effective educators—from the classroom to the central office—continually survey strengths and needs of students and strategies for building upon strengths to meet short-term and long-term needs.

CHAPTER 8

Children are the clay in the hands of the potter. The potter molds the pliable clay—gingerly shaping the image on the wheel, moistening hands frequently, trimming here, trimming there—until shape meets expectation. Firing in the kiln solidifies the image toward resilience, functionality, and permanence. And so is the molding of the capacity of the brain by the educator. "We've learned through research if you change the environment, you can change the brain."[9]

Barbara Bush reminds, "Kids want to learn. They want to stay in school. They want good jobs. They want a chance."[10] It's morning again in America. Time is fleeting. Educators have another time to be up at bat.

9

THE TRIAD

> *A small body of determined spirits fired by an unquenchable faith in their mission can alter the course of history.*[1]

The school is the nucleus of the community, of society. It is the gathering place, a place of communal ownership. Community members are parents of students. Parents of students are citizens—merchants, representatives of business and industry. The circle of ownership rolls through communities locally, nationally, and internationally. Throwing open the doors of collaboration and partnership between stakeholders in education enriches the school and capacitates robustness in the marketplace through its product—an educated citizenry.

The foundation upon which effective collaboration and vibrant partnerships—school, home, community—are established includes successful building blocks of communication.

- Talk with the person—not to him, not around her—with the individual. Maintain eye contact, an open body stance.
- Build up. Enhance dignity.

CHAPTER 9

COMMUNITY   **HOME**

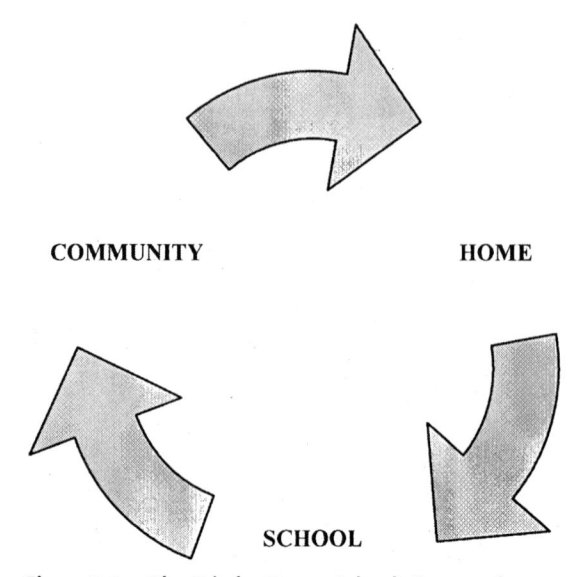

SCHOOL

Figure 9.1. The Triad—Home, School, Community

- Maintain consistency. Focus on the topic, the concern.
- Align the topic with relevance for the constituent, for the entity the constituent represents.
- Live credibility. Walk credibility. Talk credibility. Speak truth. Write truth. Quantify information.
- Incorporate multisensory illustrations for increased understanding—auditory, visual, kinesthetic.
- Listen.
- Question to determine level of understanding.
- Repeat key points. Repeat key points. Repeat key points.
- Dialogue in brief sentences, short, meaningful words.
- Initiate concepts sequentially. 1, 2, 3 may or may not equal 3, 2, 1.
- Note with whom you are speaking, with whom you are writing. Be in tune with the total person—who one is, where

one's been, what one knows, the lineage one represents, one's pain, one's joy.[2]

As children enter the classroom, their ancestors, their inheritance, familial experiences, generational traditions enter with them. To teach a child is to teach a family. To teach a family is to teach a neighborhood. To teach a neighborhood is to teach a culture. The kaleidoscope of cultures is vivid for me through my first-generation immigrant grandparents—is vivid for me through my early school years in Japan—is vivid for me through my impressionable middle school years thirty miles north of the Rio Grande in the delta through which it meanders into the Gulf of Mexico.

To forget one's ancestors is to be a brook without a source, a tree without a root.[3]

The kaleidoscope of a community encompasses socioeconomic status, ethnicities, and cultures among the vibrant colors in its prism. Individual uniqueness enriches mutual interdependence. Diversities in the foothills of the Dakotas impact tumbleweed-strewn prairies of west Texas; diversities in the lobster industry in frigid waters of Bar Harbor impact barrios of Southern California. Diversities in this nation affect the renminbi in the People's Republic of China. The renminbi in China influences the ruble in Russia. Interconnectivity through diversity encircles the globe.

Global interconnectivity through diversity is the twenty-first-century learning community. Effective teachers capture learning opportunities for all children. Effective teachers celebrate diversity. Effective teachers greet each student equitably. Effective teachers sharpen their axes of research-based instructional strategies. Effective teachers radiate high expectations for all. Effective teachers welcome—embrace—partnerships with families, partnerships with business and industry on behalf of young people.

CHAPTER 9

THE HOME

With a quiver in her voice my secretary stated that the telephone call was for me. "Good morning, this is Patricia Parrish." The voice responded, "You are not to return to my home without prior approval. I've thought again about your appearing at my front door yesterday unannounced. I don't like it." She hung up. She was right. I was wrong.

Her son, because of health conditions, was receiving instruction temporarily in his home. It was within my job description to supervise this instructional process and setting. The teacher was hired. The schedule was established.

I planned during the third week of this instructional arrangement to conduct an on-site observation unannounced. This intent was placed on my calendar. It was in the best interest of the district to maintain a close surveillance of this ticking time bomb. The parent frequently entered her son's classroom at will, dominating time and attention of staff. She presented at offices of the principal and superintendent without prior scheduled appointments, vividly ranting her dissatisfactions with services her son was receiving. The ruckus could be heard throughout the buildings. Her vocabulary rivaled any heard at the local bar.

The morning of the planned observation I located the small, white-frame house on a less traveled street. I parked at the front gate, partially ajar. It squeaked—grinding, scraping—as it dragged the surface of the broken, uneven sidewalk. I opened it enough to warily enter the untended postage-stamp yard, being particularly careful not to hang my clothing on exposed wires. I stepped cautiously up the jagged steps, weeds sprouting from the cracks. I raised my hand to knock on the screen door with holes big enough for a small pet to walk back and forth.

She was standing at the door, watching my every stumbling move. I greeted her, explaining my interest in the instructional

THE TRIAD

services her son was receiving. She unlatched the hook without a word. I walked in. She positioned herself on the lumpy sofa, covered with a faded bedspread. A distinct, stale odor tickled my nostrils. She did not speak.

The teacher courteously greeted me, encouraging the child to do so, also. She briefly demonstrated strategies being implemented. The little boy responded amicably to her efforts. The parent's silence thundered through the small room. After my feeble, unsuccessful efforts to initiate communication with her, I dismissed myself. She did not move from the lumpy sofa.

She was right. I was wrong. I had entered her culture, her world, her haven uninvited. I had violated her rituals. I was not welcome there—the lessons we learn along the way.

Building bridges, building partnerships, with families is a fragile process. The child is the glue that solidifies the structure. We come to school for children. We reach for their families, just as they are. We extend the hand of unity, of trust, on behalf of their child—their most treasured gift. In time, generally, with gentle persistence and patience, the partnership structure strengthens.

All may not be well, however, in the wigwam. More than 13 million children (one in six) live in poverty. Almost half of this number lives in extreme poverty—at less than half of the federal poverty level. (The 2009 federal poverty level is $22,050 total annual income for a family of four.) Every thirty-three seconds each day in this nation a child is born in poverty—2,583 a day. Some 1.7 million more children live in poverty today than at the turn of the century—an increase of 15 percent. Children living in poverty are less healthy, typically developmentally below age level.[4] Poor children are one-and-one-half times more likely to be identified with a disability.[5]

Designated antecedents of developmental delay, lack of school readiness, and ill health may be prevented or decreased through services funded by the federal government. Educators are

CHAPTER 9

messengers to families about these available sources of assistance. Pause a moment. When a student represents poverty, do you initiate communication with the family about services for which it may be eligible? Is this information included in newsletters to parents at the beginning of the year, during the year, when a migrant student enrolls in school? Reconsider your role in relaying information to parents about resources available in the community.

- Head Start
- Women, Infants, and Children (WIC)
- Early Childhood Intervention (ECI)
- Early Periodic Screening, Diagnosis, and Treatment (EPSDT)
- Children's Health Insurance Program (CHIP)
- Local, county, and state agencies

Established families may live generation after generation in the same neighborhood, or families may move several times during a school year through migrant labor. Schedule conferences with families in the schoolhouse. Schedule conferences in the community. Schedule conferences before school. Schedule conferences during planning periods. Schedule conferences after school. Schedule conferences with families.

Farm laborers toil in the field from daylight to dark during harvest. Butchers in the packing plant work 24/7 shifts. Truck drivers haul loads thousands of miles, returning home periodically. Flexibility by educators is critical. Parents are inherently interested in their children. They, also, are driven to put beans on the table. Lack of availability of the parents may indicate they are functioning in survival mode—another message for educators about the stress within some (many) homes of children.

Schedule parent trainings. Teach parents reading skills, computational skills, school readiness skills for their children. Schedule English classes for parents who do not speak English. Schedule trainings on school property. Schedule trainings at community sites. Provide child care. Build trainers of trainers empowering parents to train parents. Schedule parent trainings.

Tribulations associated with poverty overlap ethnicity, migrancy, language, culture. Migrant streams in the nation follow general movement and income patterns—valuable planning information for educators.

> Workers along the East Coast travel throughout Florida and other Atlantic coast states; workers in the Midwest travel largely in Texas, Ohio, Michigan, and Indiana. A third stream of workers travels along the West Coast. According to the United States Department of Labor, the median income for a farm worker household in the 21st century is $15,000–$17,499.[6]

In addition to monetary struggles, a piercing, never-ending pain parents may experience is grieving—grieving for what may have been, grieving for loss that can never be recovered, grieving for shattered dreams (and shattered bodies). As parents approach the conference with their child's teacher, they may feel incomprehensible love, guilt, grief, poverty, loneliness, homelessness, uncertainty, hope, belief, ignorance, joy, knowledge, blame.

> Our oldest child had sixteen surgeries prior to six years of age. She has spent approximately four months of her life in the hospital. She was a patient in neonatal intensive care her first five weeks. We have paid about $60,000.00 out-of-pocket medical expenses since she was born. She is now nine years old. We have dealt with some challenges.[7]

The emotions are endless. They come with the package—the package of parenthood. For some parents an added component of their package is English is their second language, if they speak any English at all.

CHAPTER 9

In the ten years between 1996 and 2006 the nation's K–12 English Language Learner population rose by over 60 percent . . . the fastest growth has taken place in parts of the country that have had little or no prior experience serving ELLs. . . . The K–12 population of . . . Nebraska and North Carolina rose by 301 and 372 percent respectively from 1996 to 2006.[8]

An urgent necessity in public schools today is building bridges with parents, navigating together through myriad hurdles of twenty-first-century childhood, culminating in productive adulthood. Success characteristics of effective bridge building, success characteristics of effective school-home conferences include, but are not limited to, the following.

- The parent speaks first. After initial greetings, the parent speaks first. Listen. Reflect on meetings in which you have been a participant. Identify sequentially the time position in which parents' input was solicited. Weigh the impact of this position. Were they first to speak—or last?
- Include an interpreter when English is the second language of the parent.
- Establish the parent as the long-term expert about the child. Presence of professionals in the life of the student is temporary. Parenthood is lifelong.
- Begin with the positive. End with the positive. Interject positive comments, providing definitive examples. Emphasize that the student demonstrates more strengths than weaknesses. Identify strengths.
- Quantify concerns. For example, "Eduardo was tardy to class seven times within a two-week time period."
- Listen.
- Correlate behaviors exhibited in school with behaviors in the home. Assess together the impact of behaviors on family members.

- Learn of recent changes in the home (i.e., birth of sibling).
- Listen.
- Speak in brief, definitive, jargon-free sentences. Breathe deeply.
- Paraphrase parents' comments, concerns, questions. Request clarification.
- Listen.
- Discuss strategies and routines parents have implemented in the home. Assess their effectiveness.
- Discuss procedures that have been implemented in school. Assess their effectiveness.
- Listen.
- Together establish strategies, routines, and procedures that will be implemented in the classroom and in the home. Build a formative monitoring schedule to collaboratively assess their effectiveness.
- Exercise caution in projecting improvement during a designated time period. Speak realistically with ample parameters for the unknown.
- Ask, "Do you have what you need? How may I assist?"
- Listen.
- Investigate available community services, resources the family may be accessing—or not accessing.
- Schedule the next conference at a mutually agreeable time and location.
- Practice, model that "it takes a village to raise a child."[9]

THE COMMUNITY

States, districts, schools, and education leaders must continue to focus on adopting a new model of learning for the 21st century. We must build on the current framework of core subjects and assessment to create an effective overall education strategy that

CHAPTER 9

equips students with 21st century skills they will need to succeed in the modern workplace.[10]

The community is an untapped powerhouse of wealth in expertise, experience, resources, and partnerships with public schools. The school is the community. The community is the school. Effective schools include representatives from the community on advisory councils vertically and horizontally throughout school-wide operations. Master craftsmen and industry leaders are silver bullets that connect the student population of today with employers in twenty-first-century occupations of tomorrow. Teamwork among the school, the community, agencies, and postsecondary institutions is actualized through strong strategic alliances that include, but are not limited to, the following.

- Speakers from business and industry—small, family-owned Mom and Pop shops to globally positioned manufacturing plants—in assemblies, parent-teacher organizations, and other school gatherings
- Concurrent and dual credit student enrollment in high school and in colleges/universities simultaneously
- Mentoring stations in the workplace in career clusters of student interest
- Articulation agreements between school district and colleges/universities in selected priority occupations
- Panels, during student and staff trainings, of local, state, and federal agency representatives in which community resources and career opportunities in designated agencies are addressed
- Senior citizen, grandparent tutors for Teddys on *every* campus
- Job shadowing, tours in multiples of employment areas in local businesses and industry
- Paid part-time employment for students enrolled in work/study programs

THE TRIAD

- Professional development focusing on twenty-first-century priority occupations presented by local business leaders
- Documented volunteering in the community by high school students as a prerequisite for graduation, scheduled volunteer activities of students at all grade levels
- Recognition of civic club representatives, firefighters, police officers in schoolwide breakfasts/lunches

I can see it from here—total participatory school and community commitment—the butcher, the baker, the candlestick maker—on behalf of *all* children of today and on behalf of a productive citizenry tomorrow. I want to go there. I want to be employed in this school. I want to be enrolled as a student. Such revolutions in public school operations entice students to come to school, to stay in school, to graduate, to march forth as productive citizens strategically equipped for successful adulthood and twenty-first-century employment.

An administrative colleague and I scheduled an appointment with the team leader representing Phillips Petroleum Company. He was a large gentleman, filled the seat completely—positioned on the other side of the long, rectangular table. "And how may I help you today?"

My colleague and I responded we came as ambassadors from the school to build alliances with local business and industry, the purpose being development of courses and career pathways based upon current and projected labor market needs. The representative was cordially intrigued with the notion, offering an on-site tour of the plant. We adjourned thereafter with the mutual commitment to continue our dialogue in the near future. My colleague and I concurrently scheduled appointments with management personnel representing Dow Chemical Company and BASF (Baden Aniline and Soda Factory).

Global sales of Dow Chemical Company are approximately $57 billion annually with 46,000 employees worldwide. Manufacturing

CHAPTER 9

sites are located in thirty-five countries.[11] BASF is the largest chemical company worldwide with sites located in thirty-four countries in Europe; thirteen countries in North America, Central America, and the Caribbean; twelve countries in South America; six countries in Africa; and twenty-seven countries in Asia/Asia Pacific. The BASF Group employs 97,000 around the globe.[12] Total student enrollment of the local school district was approximately 2,000—prekindergarten through grade 12.

It was the goal of the district to align course offerings with and through Brazosport College to meet twenty-first-century workplace needs of business and industry in the Gulf Coast region. Initial meetings were held with leadership staff of the college, resulting in a unified impetus for both educational institutions—the local school district and postsecondary education.

Subsequent planning sessions occurred with administrative representation from Brazosport College, BASF Group, Phillips Petroleum Company, Dow Chemical Company, and the local school district. It was the consensus of this planning team that the priority employment need in the region was process technology. Through multiples of sessions a seamless course of study resulted, extending from grade nine through the sophomore year in the college.

Upon completion of the associate's degree the participating student was prepared for and eagerly welcomed into employment in one of the three member industries. Students were encouraged to complete the bachelor's degree and graduate degrees during employment to increase their capacity for advancement in the industry and to increase capacity of participating industries for qualified employees who are indeed lifelong twenty-first-century learners.

It was my responsibility to coordinate and chair these strategic planning sessions. Through this collaboration between education and business and industry, instructors were shared, facilities were shared, and resources were shared—cost, time, employee efficient for each participating institution. The district was thereafter awarded the Gulf Coast Education That Works Tech Prep Excellence Award for outstanding performance in promoting tech prep, a federally funded school-to-work transition program.

This process can occur in every district in this nation. Neither the twenty-first-century school nor the twenty-first-century marketplace can longer endure continuing to do what we've always done. Regrettably, we will "get what we've always got"—a dropout rate of one-third to one-half of students in this nation devoid of employability and survival skills.

Taxpayers of this nation have had enough. Citizens are dazed by the double whammy of the revolving door as children whose education they have funded enter adulthood illiterate, unskilled, and ill equipped to survive rigors of the competitive twenty-first-century international marketplace. Applications for federally funded subsistence programs are completed by these individuals (and their children and grandchildren), adding to the tax burden of citizens in this nation. With all of the ills of society, the buck stops here—in the school. Education is the key to breaking the cycle of poverty, unemployment, and depravation.

Credibility in public education escalates when educators—*every* educator from the classroom to the central office—accepts *total* responsibility for building a defensible and defendable product—an educated citizenry. Dr. Peter Senge reminds educators, families, and business and industry—the triad . . .

> A simple question to ask is, "How has the world changed in the last 150 years?" And the answer is, "It's hard to imagine any way in which it hasn't changed."[13]

Effective educators are poised with strategic, revolutionary educational reform to spearhead this visionary imagination into

CHAPTER 9

a reality. Do you want to go there? Reform in public education is a national emergency.

- Are you the educator you want to be?
- Are you the educator you planned to be—when you entered the profession?
- Are you the educator who every day—*every day*—sharpens the axe of excellence in your classroom, in your school, in your district?
- Are you a calculated warrior toward production of an educated citizenry?

Imagine the brilliance of educators across this land—from the classroom to the central office—hand in hand with home and community reaching for and stretching to actualization of blazing, bold, data-based, accountable goals on behalf of young people, on behalf of this nation, on behalf of civilization upon this planet.

Do you want to go there?

10

A NEW ORDER

It ought to be remembered that there is nothing more difficult to take in hand, more perilous to conduct or more uncertain in its success than to take the lead in the introduction of a new order of things.[1]

A new order begins deep within an individual, deep within an institution, deep within a concept, deep within an idea. A new order sees that which may never have been seen before—imagines that which may never have been imagined (nor spoken) before—poises for that which may never have been before—as Michelangelo saw, imagined, poised as marble was transformed into civilization's beloved David. As I stood in awe near the feet of Michelangelo's David in Florence, Italy, I attempted to comprehend the vision of this artisan giant as his imagination catapulted from a nondescript boulder of marble into the prodigious David—an extraordinary portrayal of the boundlessness of human capacity.

The expert educator imagines the limitless capability of every student and poises daily, believing every child can learn. And the march begins—hand in hand—educator and student. The new order leads the drum-roll cadence of high expectations for every child.

CHAPTER 10

Expert educators from the classroom to the central office know when children are learning, teachers are teaching. When teachers are teaching, instructional leaders (principals) are instructionally leading. When instructional leaders are leading, educational leaders (superintendents) are educationally leading. The buck stops here—in educational institutions—in schools.

The proactive school is now poised, is armed for the new order. The proactive school knows to continue doing what we've always done is timeworn and threadbare.

> Our education system has been fundamental to our success as a nation, but the way we prepare students has barely changed in 100 years.[2]

No institution in this nation—other than public schools—survives when 30 to 50 percent of its products fall by the wayside during production—without meeting minimum competitive standards for the marketplace.

Components of the visionary twenty-first-century school—the new order—are submitted as the unquivering foundation for—and solid stepping-stones to—schools that work, schools in which every—every—child learns. Designated cited concepts may be considerations that have only briefly entered the deepest recesses of our thinking—may be ideas whose time for action is emerging. As committed stakeholders of educational institutions in unison march forward from "yes, but" to "what if," the lighthouse of civilization—the public school—shines brightly, and indeed it is morning again in America.

THE NEW ORDER

- The new order competes with business and industry to inspire the brightest, the most energetic, the goal-focused into education; spirals salaries upward enticing current and

future chief executive officers to employ their leadership skills in school leadership positions.
- The new order advertises nationally for dynamic campus instructional leaders who envision and are committed to leading blue-ribbon schools, holds their feet to the fire—to make calculable decisions based upon student needs and empowers these leaders to reinvent the school into a twenty-first-century learning institution with research-based instructional initiatives that result in increased student achievement.
- The new order establishes advisory councils at campus and district levels representative of community demographics, business and industry, parents of enrolled students, postsecondary education, campus and district staff, agency representatives, and students.

Advisory councils are bestowed with responsibilities to create campus and district mission statements, conduct needs assessments, build action plans with timelines, establish formative and summative evaluations, realign goals and objectives based upon evaluation findings, and designate individuals responsible for execution of the plan. Trends are defined. Through advisement of the councils, instructional programs, as applicable, are restructured based upon findings.
- The new order implements scheduled professional development based primarily at the campus level, puts the paintbrush in their hand—integrating distance learning, online learning, face-to-face learning, on-site observations of exemplary campuses, campuswide mentoring, and trainer-of-trainers models.
- The new order establishes an evaluation system and subsequent pay scale for teachers based upon sustained improvement in student achievement, professional development leadership, completion of graduate degrees, vertical and horizontal curricular collaboration, state and national professional

CHAPTER 10

organizational membership and leadership, documented participation in research-based initiatives (i.e., instructional and assessment strategies representative of higher-level thinking, quality questioning, differentiated instruction, priority occupation and marketplace skills awareness, and technology applications).

- The new order terminates teachers who retire in spirit prior to retiring physically, identifying those who present daily at the schoolhouse counting days until their first retirement pension, whose productivity has declined to the extent that revival of the spirit is unlikely.

If the flame is flickering, extinguish the candle. Maintain in the ranks of the committed only those vividly described by John Steinbeck as he reflects on effective teachers through whom he had learned.

> They all loved what they were doing. They did not tell—they catalyzed a burning desire to know. Under their influence, the horizons sprung wide and fear went away and the unknown became knowable. But most of all, the truth, that dangerous stuff, became beautiful and precious.[3]

- The new order establishes collaborative alliances with postsecondary education for alternative certification options, capturing degreed workers in other professions for classroom teaching positions.
- The new order integrates on-site mentoring for new teachers, including mandatory training institutes designed to retain the brightest in the nation in classrooms.
- The new order designs consistent, timely, districtwide face-to-face, online, hard copy, radio and television communications with all stakeholders, highlighting campus and district educational programs, auxiliary services, success of all stu-

dents at all grade levels in academics, in the arts, in athletics, in UIL competition, in service clubs and service learning, in career and technology education, in foreign language, and in other areas.

The new order includes community awareness accountability in evaluation criteria of the district superintendent, central office staff, campus instructional leaders, and classroom teachers. The new order conducts formative evaluations of resulting increase in parental involvement.

- The new order encourages business and industry, community members, agency representatives, postsecondary education, and families to actively volunteer in educational programs and services.

　　Volunteers may . . .

1. read to small groups of students,
2. mentor struggling students,
3. host job shadowing and tours in local businesses,
4. plant and tend gardens on school property,
5. lead the pledge of allegiance to the flag,
6. teach song lyrics in foreign languages,
7. greet parents and students upon moving into the neighborhood,
8. decorate halls in seasonal displays,
9. lead classes in the Mexican hat dance,
10. staff parent-friendly, child-friendly gathering locations for parents awaiting scheduled appointments with educators,
11. instruct parents with limited English in their new language,
12. prepare foods in celebration of national holidays of foreign countries,

13. file books and other materials in school libraries,
14. eat lunch with students in school cafeterias,
15. host brunches in honor of educators,
16. usher guests arriving for school assemblies.

- The new order commits that every student will demonstrate saleable skills upon graduation, includes priority occupations and twenty-first-century workplace skills in annual professional development for all teachers—prekindergarten through grade twelve, incorporates developmentally appropriate transition-to-work instructional activities—including career awareness and career counseling—at every grade level, partners with business and industry and with postsecondary education for alignment of course offerings and training programs with current and projected labor market trends.
- The new order forms alliances with local, state, and federal nonprofit organizations and agencies for canvassing neighborhoods to provide awareness of and assistance in application processes for programs for which families may be eligible, including health care services.
- The new order reviews alternative strategies in funding school facilities with state and local revenue—appropriates federal monies as available, conducts quantitative and qualitative analysis of facilities within district boundaries, projects student growth, compares growth with quantity and condition of occupied and vacant facilities.

  1. Weighs pros and cons of facilities options, including, but not limited to, lease/purchase of unoccupied structures—updating for compliance with building codes, Americans with Disabilities Act, and other factors, renovation to accommodate designated school needs (i.e., food services, school bus access).

2. Reassesses use of current school buildings toward maximum student achievement (i.e., conversion of teacher lounges into classrooms).
3. Increases salaries of district and campus faculty and staff to competitive levels with monies saved from realignment of facilities needs and options.

- The new order trains every staff member in characteristics of positive organizational climate, including proactive behavior management, ensures environment of mutual dignity for each individual, includes success characteristics from business and industry, incorporates positive school climate components in evaluation criteria of every employee.
- The new order implements razor-sharp, definitively documented, accountable, twenty-first-century educational programming for every child—every child—districtwide.

    1. Offers year-round school as a calendar option at all grade levels.
    2. Funds developmentally based, language-rich public preschool for all children as an early-start choice at the discretion of individual parents, distributes child-find communication districtwide in languages represented in district demographics.

        a. Includes active parental participation and collaboration in preschool education (i.e., home visits, parent trainings focusing on developmental milestones and school readiness activities, classroom and community-based volunteer opportunities).
        b. Conducts longitudinal study of participants, realigning curricula and additional program components based upon findings.

c. Provides after-school developmentally appropriate reinforcement and enrichment instructional services based on sliding-scale fee paid by participating parents.

- The new order instills and expects a school environment based on Dr. Tony Wagner's seven survival skills: critical thinking, collaboration, adaptability, entrepreneurialism, effective communication, analysis, and imagination.[4]
- The new order creates a technology-based educational environment including, but not limited to, global-age software and hardware, global-age instructional activities, and global-age expertise of faculty and staff, subsequently linking technology proficiency to evaluations of administrative and instructional employees.
- The new order offers districtwide programs for students who demonstrate giftedness.

  1. Includes, but is not limited to, enrichment programs, accelerated instruction, advanced placement, international baccalaureate curricula.
  2. Establishes eligibility from multiples of sources (i.e., mathematics, linguistic, arts, leadership).
  3. Maintains keen astuteness of giftedness from poverty populations and from each ethnicity represented in student demographics.

- The new order designs a staff position whose primary role is building seamless steps from graduation to entry into meaningful employment and/or postsecondary enrollment, includes responsibilities for researching scholarships, grants, and loans for graduating seniors based upon strengths and upon apparent need, builds connectivity with postsecondary personnel for graduates entering selected colleges and

A NEW ORDER

universities, enlists community volunteers and staff to mentor through the transition process.

Walter was a gifted child. I first became acquainted with him when he was a little boy playing baseball in the local little league. I was mesmerized as he communicated—years beyond his age. Walter entered kindergarten with already developed skills in reading.

I began early to discuss with him his apparent skills and aptitude, the benefits of maintaining focus academically for present and future opportunities awaiting him. Even as a young child it was apparent an academic scholarship upon graduation was likely. Through each school year he demonstrated intellectual and academic prowess. With eagerness he and I discussed multiples of universities to which he may apply. As he neared graduation his application packets included letters of recommendation I had written for him.

Papa worked at the plant. Mama fulfilled many, many household responsibilities well. Each was a graduate of local high schools. Initiation of communication about the apparent giftedness of their older son brought quizzical looks, nothing more. Walter was years older than his siblings—a blended family. Needs of the younger children demanded their parents' time, attention, and energy. The quizzical looks resulted in minimal subsequent conversation about the remarkable intellectual capacity of their older son, Walter.

Walter secured a full scholarship to one of the most prestigious universities in the nation. I rejoiced with him, and thereafter he moved hundreds of miles away. Upon questioning years later about Walter, I learned he arrived on campus, settled into his dorm, minimally attended classes—a foreigner in a strange land—a university campus.

Multiples of communications of concern from the university were unheeded by Mama and Papa. They didn't come to

CHAPTER 10

his rescue. They didn't understand the arena in which their older son was now attempting to survive. They didn't know the fragility of the first semester in an institution of higher learning in a distant city.

After the first semester Walter's full scholarship was withdrawn. He returned home.

Walter works at the plant.

We may step back. We may look away, shuffling our feet, clearing out throat, lowering our eyes. We may declare we cannot take on all of the children we have known—all of the children of the world. I submit another way of thinking. We are our brother's keeper. They are all our children. This is a truism of the universe—from one generation to the next. We are our brother's keeper. Failure to help the gifted child reach his potential is a personal tragedy, is a societal tragedy, the extent of which is difficult to measure.

- The new order signs articulation agreements with postsecondary education, develops dual credit course offerings, encourages concurrent enrollment in the local high school and in postsecondary education.
- The new order integrates foreign language in district curricula beginning in prekindergarten—enriching participation in the multicultural society of the twenty-first century, embellishing the globally competitive edge of graduates.
- The new order implements a no-frills, quantitative-based, no-excuses, zero-tolerance dropout prevention and reentry initiative extending from prekindergarten through grade twelve.
    1. Identifies students in prekindergarten and each grade thereafter who are at risk for dropping out of high school—the English language learners, those living in poverty, the homeless, those whose home is print de-

ficient, those functioning below grade level, migrants, the frequently absent, discipline referrals, minority populations, and additional at-risk indicators.
2. Includes dropout prevention and reentry initiatives in district and campus action plans, designating persons responsible, allocating resources, timelines, formative and summative evaluations.
3. Includes early detection of at-risk indicators with accompanying intervention strategies, prison population data, and earnings comparisons of high school graduates and high school dropouts in campus and district professional development.

   a. Thirty percent of federal inmates, 40 percent of state prison inmates, and 50 percent of persons on death row are high school dropouts.
   b. Annual income for individuals who drop out of high school is approximately $21,000. Annual income for high school graduates is $31,400.[5]

4. Establishes campus-based teams *at every grade level* for monitoring demonstrated at-risk characteristics, includes subsequent interventions, develops cross-sectional and longitudinal studies of campus and district initiatives, realigns initiatives based upon findings.
5. Builds strong bridges with parents early in the school career of students, scheduling parent trainings at every grade level about school success characteristics, priority occupations, twenty-first-century workplace skills, postsecondary education opportunities and procedures.
6. Organizes teams of volunteers, including school personnel, to contact prior dropouts and their families offering mentorship upon reentry of the dropout into the school environment.

7. Implements innovative instructional program options for returning dropouts in buildings separate from or with traditional students, offers instruction at varied times (mornings, afternoons, evenings, weekends), includes child care for returning participants, employs on-site transition counselors as returning dropouts acclimate to the instructional environment and as successful graduates transition to postsecondary education and/or the workforce, provides online course options.
8. Schedules preparation sessions, including transition counseling, for the GED (General Educational Development) in multiples of locations in the community at varying times (mornings, afternoons, evenings, weekends) with child care provisions for participants.
9. Develops a tracking process with accompanying monetary incentives as dropouts return to school and graduate through either course completion or GED.
10. Includes social skills training on every campus at every grade level through a buddy system—student to student, student to staff—for a total school environment of caring and responsibility for each enrolled student.
11. Implements response-to-intervention model at all grade levels with supporting program initiatives per needs and eligibilities of individual students.
12. Includes real-world applications in instructional strategies, linking strategies to teacher and administrator evaluations.
13. Analyzes short-term and long-term impact of retention.

Grade retention is one of the most powerful predictors of school dropout.[6]

Initiatives cited are a springboard for dynamic human synergy in institutions of public education and in communities across this land. Through comprehensive analysis and assessment of these strategies all stakeholders—the butcher, the baker, the candlestick maker, the small business owner, the international industry executive, the student, the graduate, the dropout, the parent struggling in poverty, the aristocrat bathing in affluence, the educator, the politician—will embrace where we are, where we want to go, and the rigorous pathway we must travel to reach our mutual goal—an educated citizenry equipped to function successfully in the international economy of the twenty-first century.

Through this vision of calculated unity this nation will experience the birth of a world-class educational system that will lead dynamic international change for all global citizens. No societal, structural ill is as urgent, is as far-reaching, is as gut-level penetrating as documentable, research-based accountability in public schools in this nation—*every school—every campus—every classroom.*

THE STADIUM—I CAN SEE IT NOW.

It is morning again in America. Educators have another time at bat. The stadium of humanity is filled to capacity; seats are occupied by stakeholders from all nationalities of the world, from every socioeconomic level. I can see it now.

Parents weep in jubilation. The national institution of hope—the national institution that is the level playing field for all students—red, yellow, black, and white (and brown?)!—the school—is in the agony of rebirth—to a higher level, to a new order, to a total commitment to indeed equip every student for the rigorous, treacherous, unforgiving demands of the twenty-first century. The crowds applaud in anticipation.

The community—business and industry—jumps to its feet in unbridled exhilaration that educational institutions at last comprehend that schools must launch from its portals empowered graduates with competitive, saleable skills that ensure marketplace

CHAPTER 10

robustness in the free enterprise system in this nation. With this strategic foundation for graduates and the cutting edge for business and industry, the United States of America will regain its prowess, its prominence, and its stability in the international arena of the twenty-first century, the twenty-second century, and beyond. The crowds applaud in exhilaration.

The students are entering the stadium now, acknowledging, truly believing, that education is the gateway—the only equitable gateway any civilization has ever imagined and developed—to the American dream—to freedom. I see them now—red, yellow, black, and white (and brown?)!. They're coming—right, left—the poor, the wealthy, the slow learner, the gifted, the downtrodden, the homeless—all our children. The crowds applaud, truly believing.

In the distance I see the ones who got away—the fallen—the dropouts. They're turning around now, squinting, trying to believe—could it be true?—that indeed this raging reformation in public schools will equip them with real-world skills for survival and success in their neighborhoods, in their communities, in their state, in their nation. Did we—stakeholders in educational institutions, each citizen of the global society—see when they left our classrooms, our hallways, when they drifted away? Did we even notice the void their absence represented and represents—the dropouts—the void—in the school, in the community, in the workplace?

Every school day in America more than 2,000 students drop out of high school, walk out the door prior to graduation—a societal, national waste—a societal, national disgrace—a societal, national tragedy.[7]

It is morning again in America.

Educators have another time at bat.

The crowd is hushed now.

Constituents of schools—citizens of the world—peer toward the playing field—the school—silent—watchfully waiting, expecting.

It is morning again in America.

A NEW ORDER

Today—now—this moment—it is your turn—it is my turn—to step up to the plate—to do what we know we must do—to be the educator we want to be—to be the educator we expected to be when we entered the profession—to activate best practices and research-based strategies every day in every classroom in this nation.

I'll meet you there.

NOTES

CHAPTER 1

1. Poverty in the United States. (n.d.). Retrieved from http://en.wikipedia.org/wiki/Poverty_in_the_United_States.
2. Smith, D. D. (2007). *Introduction to special education: Making a difference,* 6th ed. Boston: Allyn and Bacon, 93.
3. "Ed Sec'y Duncan bemoans 30 percent dropout rate." (September 8, 2009). Retrieved from http://www.breitbart.com/article.php?id=D9AJ35J04&show_article=1.
4. Poverty in the United States. (n.d.). Retrieved from http://en.wikipedia.org/wiki/Poverty_in_the_United_States.
5. "What it takes to make a student." (November 26, 2006). Retrieved from http://www.nytimes.com/2006/11/26/magazine/26tough.html?pagewanted=2&_r=2.

CHAPTER 2

1. Schools and staffing survey. (2000–2008). National Center for Education Statistics. Retrieved from http://nces.ed.gov/surveys/sass/tables_list.asp.

NOTES

2. "Nation's population one-third minority." (May 10, 2006). Retrieved from http://www.census.gov/Press-Release/www/releases/archives/population/006808.html.
3. Hood, E. C. (personal communication, 1976).
4. Bloom's Taxonomy Verbs. (2000–2007). Pearson Education, Inc. Retrieved from http://www.teachervision.fen.com/curriculum-planning/printable/52434.html.
5. Farwell, S. (October 16, 2005). "Dallas at the tipping point: An update." *Dallas Morning News*, 1.

CHAPTER 3

1. Problems. (April 2, 2009). Retrieved from http://www.giga-usa.com/quotes/topics/problems_t001.htm.
2. Texas Education Code, Sections 11.251, 11.252, 11.253.
3. Burnett, F. H. (1962). *Secret garden*, 3rd copyright renewal. Philadelphia: J. B. Lippincott Company, 242.

CHAPTER 4

1. Murphy, J. D. (2005). *Flawless execution*. New York: HarperCollins Publishers, Inc., 184.
2. Glickman, C. "Leadership for learning: How to help teachers succeed." Schmoker, M. (February 2004). *Tipping point: From feckless reform to substantive instructional improvement*. Phi Delta Kappan, 424–32.
3. Collins, J. (2001). *Good to great: Why some companies make the leap . . . and others don't*. New York: HarperCollins Publishers, Inc., 62.
4. Author unknown. "We will stand by each other like that!"

CHAPTER 5

1. Bryant, B. (personal communication, 1994).
2. Woolfolk, A. (2007). *Educational psychology*, 10th ed. Boston: Allyn and Bacon, 96.

NOTES

3. Quaid, L. (2009). "1 in 4 drops out of high school, but some cities improve." Retrieved from http://www.usatoday.com/news/education/2009-04-23-dropouts-high-school_N.htm?loc=interstitialskip.

4. Bloom's Taxonomy verbs. (2000-2007). Pearson Education, Inc. Retrieved from http://www.teachervision.fen.com/curriculum-planning/printable/52434.html.

5. Lambert, L. (May 9, 2006). "Half of teachers quit in 5 years." Retrieved from http://www.washingtonpost.com/wp-dyn/content/article/2006/05/08/AR2006050801344.html.

6. Schlechty, P. C. (2002). *Working on the work: An action plan for teachers, principals, and superintendents.* San Francisco: Jossey-Bass, 45–52.

CHAPTER 6

1. From the memory of the author. "The Rainbow."

2. Languages in the United States. Retrieved from http://academic kids.com/encyclopedia/index.php/Languages_in_the_United_States.

3. Smith, D. D. (2007). *Introduction to special education: Making a difference*, 6th ed. Boston: Allyn and Bacon, 80.

4. Hendricks, T. (March 14, 2005). "Bay area report: 112 languages spoken in diverse region." Retrieved from http://www.sfgate.com/cgi bin/article.cgi?f=/c/a/2005/03/14/BAG2CBOTOP1.DTL.

5. Woolfolk, A. (2007). *Educational psychology*, 10th ed. Boston: Allyn and Bacon, 162.

6. Woolfolk, A. (2007). *Educational psychology*, 10th ed. Boston: Allyn and Bacon, 162.

7. Taylor, M. D. (1976). *Roll of thunder, hear my cry.* New York: Dial Press.

8. Each day in America for all children. Children's Defense Fund. Retrieved from www.childrensdefense.org.

9. U.S. Department of Health and Human Services. "Women's health USA 2008." Retrieved from http://mchb.hrsa.gov/whusa08/.

10. The research appears in: Smith, D. D. (2004). *Introduction to special education: Making a difference*, 5th ed. Boston: Allyn and Bacon, 230.

NOTES

11. Reis, S. M. "Research that supports the need for and benefits of gifted education." Retrieved from www.supradotati.ro/resurse/Benefits-of-Gifted-Edu-NAGC.pdf.

12. Parrish, L. J. (personal communication, circa 1990).

13. "The twice-exceptional dilemma." (2006). National Education Association. Retrieved from http://www.cflparents.org/Information/Resources/PublicSchool/TwiceExceptional.pdf.

14. Thompson-Cannino, J., Cotton, R., Torneo, E. (2009). *Picking cotton: Our memoir of injustice and redemption.* New York: St. Martin's Press.

15. Hughes, I. M. (October 1990). "We are responsible for children." *School Psychology.*

CHAPTER 7

1. Covey, S. R. (1990). *The 7 habits of highly effective people.* New York: Simon & Schuster, 97.

2. Source of fable unknown.

3. Garza, A. O. (August 28, 2009). "Antonio O. Garza: An education model that's truly local." Retrieved from http://www.dallasnews.com/sharedcontent/dws/dn/opinion/viewpoints/stories/DN-garza_31edi.State.Edition1.1d146e2.html.

4. Schlechty, P. C. (2002). *Working on the work: An action plan for teachers, principals, and superintendents.* San Francisco: Jossey-Bass, 52.

CHAPTER 8

1. Gardner, H. (May 25, 2005). "Multiple lenses on the mind." Expo-Gestion Conference, Bogotá, Colombia.

2. Reagan, R. (1984). "It's morning in America again." Retrieved from http://www.youtube.com/watch?v=EU-IBF8nwSY.

3. Arnove, R. F. (Spring 2006). "How is the global economy changing educational priorities in your country?" *Stanford Educator,* 7.

4. Downey, M. (June 15, 2009). "Are they unteachable?" *Atlanta Journal-Constitution,* 1, 2.

NOTES

5. Author unknown. "Three letters from Teddy."
6. Larson, M. E. (n.d.). "Who are the gifted?" Retrieved from http://oregonstate.edu/instruct/ed419/wgdocument.html.
7. McAnally, O. (personal communication, circa 1988).
8. Turner, W. E. (personal communication, circa 1980).
9. Peters, E. A. (June 5, 2009). "Expanding your mind not just expression." *Abilene Reporter News*, 1.
10. Bush, B. (December 14, 2009). "A precious moment." *Newsweek*, 1

CHAPTER 9

1. Gandhi, M. in Youngerman-Meyer, B. (Winter 2002). "A determined spirit." *Harvard Public Health Review*. Retrieved from www.hsph.harvard.edu/review/review_winter_02/txtalumspirit.html.
2. Luntz, F. (2007). *Words that work: It's not what you say, it's what people hear*. New York: Hyperion, 4–31.
3. Chinese proverb. Retrieved from http://thoughts.forbes.com/thoughts/ancestors-chinese-proverb-to-forget-ones.
4. Cradle to prison pipeline poverty fact sheet. (March 2009). Children's Defense Fund. Retrieved from www.childrensdefense.org.
5. Smith, D. D. (2007). *Introduction to special education: Making a difference*, 6th ed. Boston: Allyn and Bacon, 95.
6. Aguilar, E. (November 7, 2009). "Coming together for better education." *Corpus Christi Caller-Times*, 2.
7. Parrish, S. J. (personal communication, January 2010).
8. The American recovery and reinvestment act: Recommendations for addressing the needs of English language learners. (March 20, 2009). Retrieved from http://www.stanford.edu/~hakuta/ARRA/ELL%20Stimulus%20Recommendations.pdf.
9. African proverb in text of Hillary Clinton speech. (August 27, 1996). Retrieved from www.happinessonline.org/LoveAndHelpChildren/p12.htm.
10. Partnership for 21st Century Skills. (n.d.). *The 21st century skills mile guide: Creating a new model of learning*. Retrieved from www.aea1.k12.ia.us/technology/P21_MILE_GUIDE.pdf.

11. "Dow Chemical Corporation. Our company." (n.d.). Retrieved from www.dow.com/about.

12. BASF at a glance. (n.d.). Retrieved from www.basf.com.

13. Washington State Society for Human Resource Management. (n.d.). "Workforce readiness." Retrieved from http://wastatecouncil.shrm.org/webmodules/webarticlesnet/templates/?a=9&z=5.

CHAPTER 10

1. Machiavelli, N. (1515). *The prince.* Retrieved from www.design.caltech.edu/erik/Misc/Machiavelli.html.

2. Gates, B. (February 1, 2010). "A quiet revolution." *Newsweek,* 9.

3. Steinbeck, J. (n.d.). "On teaching." Retrieved from www.rjgeib.com/thoughts/truth/on-teaching.html.

4. Wagner, T. (2008). *The global achievement gap: Why even our best schools don't teach the new survival skills our children need—and what we can do about it.* New York: Basic Books.

5. National Center for Education Statistics. "Dropout rates and completion rates in the United States: 2006." Retrieved from http://nces.ed.gov/pubs2008/dropout06.

6. Jimerson, S. R., Ferguson, P., Whipple A. D., Anderson, G. E., and Dalton, M. J. (2002). "Exploring the association between grade retention and dropout: A longitudinal study examining socio-emotional, behavioral, and achievement characteristics of retained students." *The California School Psychologist,* vol. 7, 51–62.

7. Each day in America. (December 2009). Children's Defense Fund. Retrieved from www.childrensdefense.org/child-research-data-publications/each-day-in-america.html.

BIBLIOGRAPHY

African proverb in text of Hillary Clinton speech. (August 27, 1996). Retrieved from www.happinessonline.org/LoveAndHelpChildren/p12.htm.

Aguilar, E. (November 7, 2009). "Coming together for better education." *Corpus Christi Caller-Times.*

The American recovery and reinvestment act: Recommendations for addressing the needs of English language learners. (March 20, 2009). Retrieved from http://www.stanford.edu/~hakuta/ARRA/ELL%20 Stimulus%20Recommendations.pdf.

Arnove, R. F. (Spring 2006). "How is the global economy changing educational priorities in your country?" *Stanford Educator.*

Author unknown. "Three letters from Teddy."

Author unknown. "We will stand by each other like that!"

BASF at a glance. (n.d.). Retrieved from www.basf.com.

Bloom's Taxonomy Verbs. (2000–2007). Pearson Education, Inc. Retrieved from http://www.teachervision.fen.com/curriculum-planning/printable/52434.html.

Bryant, B. (personal communication, 1994).

Burnett, F. H. (1962). *Secret garden*, 3rd copyright renewal. Philadelphia: J. B. Lippincott Company.

Bush, B. (December 14, 2009). "A precious moment." *Newsweek.*

BIBLIOGRAPHY

Children's Defense Fund. Cradle to prison pipeline poverty fact sheet. (March 2009). Retrieved from www.childrensdefense.org.

Children's Defense Fund. Each day in America. (December 2009). Retrieved from www.childrensdefense.org/child-research-data-publications/each-day-in-america.html.

Chinese proverb. Retrieved from http://thoughts.forbes.com/thoughts/ancestors-chinese-proverb-to-forget-ones.

Collins, J. (2001). *Good to great: Why some companies make the leap . . . and others don't*. New York: HarperCollins Publishers, Inc.

Covey, S. R. (1990). *The 7 habits of highly effective people*. New York: Simon & Schuster.

Dow Chemical Corporation. Our company (n.d.). Retrieved from www.dow.com/about.

Downey, M. (June 15, 2009). "Are they unteachable?" *Atlanta Journal-Constitution*.

"Ed Sec'y Duncan bemoans 30 percent dropout rate." (September 8, 2009). Retrieved from http://www.breitbart.com/article.php?id=D9AJ35J04&show_article=1.

Farwell, S. (October 16, 2005). "Dallas at the tipping point: An update." *Dallas Morning News*.

From the memory of the author. "The Rainbow."

Gandhi, M. in Youngerman-Meyer, B. (Winter 2002). "A determined spirit." *Harvard Public Health Review*. Retrieved from www.hsph.harvard.edu/review/review_winter_02/txtalumspirit.html.

Gardner, H. (May 25, 2005). "Multiple lenses on the mind." ExpoGestion Conference, Bogotá, Colombia.

Garza, A. O. (August 28, 2009). "Antonio O. Garza: An education model that's truly local." Retrieved from http://www.dallasnews.com/sharedcontent/dws/dn/opinion/viewpoints/stories/DN-garza_31edi.State.Edition1.1d146e2.html.

Gates, B. (February 1, 2010). "A quiet revolution." *Newsweek*.

Glickman, C. "Leadership for learning: How to help teachers succeed," in Schmoker, M. (February 2004). *Tipping point: From feckless reform to substantive instructional improvement*. Phi Delta Kappan.

BIBLIOGRAPHY

Hendricks, T. (March 14, 2005). "Bay area report: 112 languages spoken in diverse region." Retrieved from http://www.sfgate.com/cgi-bin/article.cgi?f=/c/a/2005/03/14/BAG2CBOTOP1.DTL.

Hood, E. C. (personal communication, 1976).

Hughes, I. M. (October 1990). "We are responsible for children." *School Psychology.*

Jimerson, S. R., Ferguson, P., Whipple A. D., Anderson, G. E., and Dalton, M. J. (2002). "Exploring the association between grade retention and dropout: A longitudinal study examining socio-emotional, behavioral, and achievement characteristics of retained students." *The California School Psychologist.*

Lambert, L. (May 9, 2006). "Half of teachers quit in 5 years." Retrieved from http://www.washingtonpost.com/wp-dyn/content/article/2006/05/08/AR2006050801344.html.

Languages in the United States. Retrieved from http://academickids.com/encyclopedia/index.php/Languages_in_the_United_States.

Larson, M. E. (n.d.). "Who are the gifted?" Retrieved from http://oregonstate.edu/instruct/ed419/wgdocument.html.

Luntz, F. (2007). *Words that work: It's not what you say, it's what people hear.* New York: Hyperion.

Machiavelli, N. (1515). *The prince.* Retrieved from www.design.caltech.edu/erik/Misc/Machiavelli.html.

McAnally, O. (personal communication, circa 1988).

Murphy, J. D. (2005). *Flawless execution.* New York: HarperCollins Publishers, Inc.

Nation's population one-third minority. (May 10, 2006). Retrieved from http://www.census.gov/Press-Release/www/releases/archives/population/006808.html.

National Center for Education Statistics. "Dropout and completion rates in the United States: 2006." Retrieved from http://nces.ed.gov/pubs2008/dropout06.

National Center for Education Statistics. Schools and staffing survey. (2000–2008). Retrieved from http://nces.ed.gov/surveys/sass/tables_list.asp.

BIBLIOGRAPHY

National Education Association. "The twice-exceptional dilemma." (2006). Retrieved from www.cflparents.org/Information/Resources/PublicSchool/TwiceExceptional.pdf.

Parrish, L. J. (personal communication, circa 1990).

Parrish, S. J. (personal communication, January 2010).

Partnership for 21st Century Skills. (n.d.). *The 21st century skills mile guide: Creating a new model of learning.* Retrieved from www.aea1.k12.ia.us/technology/P21_MILE_GUIDE.pdf.

Peters, E. A. (June 5, 2009). "Expanding your mind not just expression." *Abilene Reporter News.*

Poverty in the United States. (n.d.). Retrieved from http://en.wikipedia.org/wiki/Poverty_in_the_United_States.

Problems. (April 2, 2009). Retrieved from http://www.giga-usa.com/quotes/topics/problems_t001.htm.

Quaid, L. (2009). "1 in 4 drops out of high school, but some cities improve." Retrieved from http://www.usatoday.com/news/education/2009-04-23-dropouts-high-school_N.htm?loc=interstitialskip.

Reagan, R. (1984). "It's morning in America again." Retrieved from http://www.youtube.com/watch?v=EU-IBF8nwSY.

Reis, S. M. "Research that supports the need for and benefits of gifted education." Retrieved from www.supradotati.ro/resurse/Benefits-of-Gifted-Edu-NAGC.pdf.

Schlechty, P. C. (2002). *Working on the work: An action plan for teachers, principals, and superintendents.* San Francisco: Jossey-Bass.

Smith, D. D. (2004). *Introduction to special education: Making a difference*, 5th ed. Boston: Allyn and Bacon.

Smith, D. D. (2007). *Introduction to special education: Making a difference*, 6th ed. Boston: Allyn and Bacon.

Steinbeck, J. (n.d.). "On teaching." Retrieved from www.rjgeib.com/thoughts/truth/on-teaching.html.

Taylor, M. D. (1976). *Roll of thunder, hear my cry.* New York: Dial Press.

Texas Education Code, Sections 11.251, 11.252, 11.253.

Thompson-Cannino, J., Cotton, R., Torneo, E. (2009). *Picking cotton: Our memoir of injustice and redemption.* New York: St. Martin's Press.

Turner, W. E. (personal communication, circa 1980).

BIBLIOGRAPHY

U.S. Department of Health and Human Services. "Women's health USA 2008." Retrieved from http://mchb.hrsa.gov/whusa08/.

Wagner, T. (2008). *The global achievement gap: Why even our best schools don't teach the new survival skills our children need—and what we can do about it.* New York: Basic Books.

Washington State Society for Human Resource Management. (n.d.) "Workforce readiness." Retrieved from http://wastatecouncil.shrm.org/webmodules/webarticlesnet/templates/?a=9&z=5.

"What it takes to make a student." (November 26, 2006). Retrieved from http://www.nytimes.com/2006/11/26/magazine/26tough.html?pagewanted=2&_r=2.

Woolfolk, A. (2007). *Educational psychology*, 10th ed. Boston: Allyn and Bacon.

ABOUT THE AUTHOR

Patricia Anne Duncan Parrish, EdD, completed the doctoral degree in educational administration from Texas A&M University–Commerce in 1994. She has been active in K–12 public education for more than thirty years in instructional, diagnostic, and central office administrative positions in New York and in Texas. At the present time, Dr. Parrish is an instructor in the College of Education and Human Services of Texas A&M University–Commerce. She contracts with Educational Testing Service, Princeton, New Jersey, in addition to scheduling public speaking and professional development with schools, professional organizations, and civic groups. She has authored multiples of newspaper, journal, and newsletter articles and informational brochures. Dr. Parrish was selected as a committee member for online teacher education graduate-level course development through Texas A&M University–Commerce (eCollege platform) and through the Transition to Teaching grant of Texas A&M University–College Station.

Dr. Parrish began her childhood education in Nagoya, Japan. She has attended seven universities and completed nine professional certifications in education. She is a Nationally Certified Educational Diagnostician (#0171) and is a Registered Professional

ABOUT THE AUTHOR

Educational Diagnostician (#1044) in the state of Texas. Dr. Parrish maintains membership in multiples of professional organizations, including Phi Delta Kappa, an international professional association for educators. In addition to living in Japan, Dr. Parrish has lived or traveled in each of the fifty states in the United States, in Costa Rica, in Panama, in multiples of locations in Canada, throughout Mexico, in Russia, and extensively in Europe. For additional information about the professional career of Dr. Parrish, including scheduling speaking and training engagements, visit www.edu-excellence.com.